CLEVER BLACKS,
JESUS AND NKANDLA

For Charles, Belinda, Jessica and Matthew,
who helped to foster my love for words and meaning.

CLEVER BLACKS, JESUS AND NKANDLA

THE REAL JACOB ZUMA
IN HIS OWN WORDS

GARETH VAN ONSELEN

JONATHAN BALL PUBLISHERS
JOHANNESBURG & CAPE TOWN

Originally published in South Africa in 2014 by
JONATHAN BALL PUBLISHERS (PTY) LTD
A division of Media24 Limited
PO Box 33977
Jeppestown
2043

Reprinted once in 2014

ISBN 978-1-86842-618-8
eBook ISBN 978-1-86842-619-5

Twitter: http://www.twitter.com/JonathanBallPub
Facebook: http://www.facebook.com/pages/Jonathan-Ball-Publishers/298034457992
Blog: http://jonathanball.bookslive.co.za/

Cover by Publicide
Design and typesetting by Triple M Design, Johannesburg
Printed and bound by Paarl Media, Paarl
Set in 9,5/13,5pt ITC Century Std

CONTENTS

ABOUT THE AUTHOR

Gareth van Onselen obtained a master's degree in sociology at the University of the Witwatersrand before moving to Cape Town in 2001 and working for the Democratic Alliance in South Africa's parliament. Among other things, he oversaw the party's research and communications as an executive director. He left the party in early 2013 to move into journalism. He now writes a daily column for *Business Day* and works as a senior reporter for the *Sunday Times*. Follow him on Twitter – @GvanOnselen.

INTRODUCTION

THE MAN WHO WALKS IN TWO WORLDS

Imagine a man who supported virginity testing for girls; promoted deference of women before men as a sign of respect; questioned the constitutionality of bail; claimed that gay marriage was a disgrace before God; advocated prosecuting people even when the evidence against them was insufficient; believed the political party he represented was endorsed by God and that a vote against it would send you to hell; celebrated tyrants when they perverted democracy; advocated the beating of children in the name of discipline; defended Julius Malema as a future leader and Thabo Mbeki's dissident views on HIV/Aids; argued that his party was more important than the Constitution; suggested that black people were defined by traditional African culture; believed that his party would govern until the end of days; regularly contradicted himself and reneged on his undertakings; paroled convicted criminals and defended his friendship with them; and regularly demonstrated an inability to take an ethical position on moral issues. A man who believed that all women should be married and that children were good training for womanhood; thought the Constitution granted minorities fewer rights than those in the majority; believed that pet dogs were un-African, as was the justice system, but encouraged people not to think like Africans in Africa; argued that prisons were unnecessary punishment and that crimes were better resolved through debate; was regularly corrected and reinterpreted by political handlers to make his gaffes more palatable; made unkept promises to appease whichever audience he was addressing; suggested that hair straightener was an attempt by black people to become 'white'; benefited from R250 million in public money spent on upgrading his private house; had friends who would land their private plane at a National Key Point for their own convenience; thought a shower minimised the risk of contracting HIV/Aids; and blamed the media for an exaggerated and unfair public perception of his views.

You are imagining the president of South Africa. His name is Jacob Zuma.

These, some of the many controversies Jacob Zuma has stirred in South African politics over the past decade, are the subject of this book. Each quote speaks to a controversial position held by Zuma, whether an initial remark or a further illustration of a theme. The book is about the real Jacob Zuma because, it argues, these controversial statements – far more so than the formal words that define his official duties as president – reveal the primary impulses that underpin his private convictions.

What are those convictions? Zuma is a traditionalist, powerfully influenced by a set of cultural values that often run contrary to the Bill of Rights and the constitutional principles that underpin it. He is a patriarch, who describes women as subservient to men, there to be wives and mothers. He sees himself as a father figure, a chief, with respect and deference due to him in equal measure and patronage his to reward and withdraw. Those in his favour often act with impunity as a result. He is a bigot, dismissive of homosexuality, which he believes violates God's law. He is a demagogue who plays different tunes to different audiences and who engenders the support of demagogues in return. His majoritarianism regularly clashes with the Constitution and many of its most central tenets, from the right to bail and the assumption of innocence before being proven guilty to individual liberties and rights. And his religiosity conflates church and state just as it elevates his party, the African National Congress, to divine status, beyond the reach of mortals and the free choice the Constitution grants them. Finally, he is a social conservative and a pragmatist who harbours an anti-democratic impulse about a number of issues.

His convictions are all-important, being the private backdrop to a public persona. They influence his decision-making, define his responses to problems and illustrate an agenda he is often constrained, by virtue of his constitutional obligations, from fully indulging. Understanding them allows one to go some way towards appreciating the view from his balcony.

Zuma is many other things, too. No doubt he has a number of virtues, but they have not come to define his public standing. Rather, it is his more controversial remarks that have left an indelible mark on South African public discourse. Indeed, his formal record is as bland and unremarkable as it is unexceptional. He will not be remembered as a visionary or philosopher king.

Zuma believes that much of the resultant criticism is unwarranted; that the media, which he believes often acts as an opposition party against him, is responsible for exaggerating, misrepresenting, taking his comments out of context and focusing only on the negative. But Zuma's own words form the bulk of this book. You can judge for yourself whether, collectively, they paint the picture of a misunderstood president or a traditional demagogue out of sync with the demands of a modern democracy.

His issue with the media is not entirely without justification. Often his words are twisted. Zuma has never used the term 'clever blacks', for example. What he said was that 'some Africans, who become too clever, take a position, they become the most eloquent in criticising themselves about their own traditions and everything'. Likewise, try as you might, you will find no direct quote in which Zuma says that having a pet dog is un-African. The original story in *The Mercury* reads: 'Spending money on buying a dog, taking it to the vet and for walks belonged to white culture and was not the African way, which was to focus on the family, President Jacob Zuma said in a speech in KwaZulu-Natal on Wednesday.' That is as close as you will get.

The *Sowetan* opened its story about Zuma's comment that Julius Malema had 'illustrated he was a good leader' by saying: 'Opposition parties have slammed President Jacob Zuma for suggesting the ANC Youth League leader Julius Malema is worthy of being the country's president in the future.' But Zuma never used the word 'president', although that sentiment would come to define the subsequent debate.

In all of these cases, and many others besides, Zuma is right: there was some manipulation – by the media and public alike – to ramp up the hysteria and the sensation. However, for all that, the intrinsic truth of each remark was never misrepresented, whether attributed, quoted or paraphrased. Examine almost every example: very rarely does Zuma contest the fundamental position at play. The rest is word games, with any confusion later disproved by Zuma himself, who inevitably repeats the sentiment in another form on another occasion.

The public, Zuma will be the first to tell you, is not stupid. Very quickly, its members understand the sentiment that informs a position. The phrase 'clever blacks' might not be literally accurate, but it has become a powerful metaphor, like so many other 'Zumerisms', for his attitude to this subject. Like it or not, Zuma has branded himself. Public sentiment has, more often than not, merely refined his slogans into more clinical and memorable sound bites.

Zuma engages in linguistic gymnastics to try to explain away his troubles. He has often been at pains to argue that something he said was not, in fact, what he meant. But he is almost always selective in his defence. When he said gay marriage was a disgrace before God, his apology made no attempt to address this particular statement. Rather, he focused on a secondary remark – '[w]hen I was growing up, an *ungqingili* [homosexual] would not have stood in front of me. I would knock him out' – by saying that he 'commented in particular about the manner in which communities tend to neglect the boy children and over-emphasise the traditional upbringing of girl children as evidenced in ceremonies such as the reed dance'. Of God and equality, however, he had little to say.

Zuma has become such a rhetorical liability that it is now something of a cliché when the presidential or ANC spokesperson releases a statement 'clarifying' the president's position. The public and media seem merely to note his latest fumbling, waiting instead to take issue with the spin doctoring that will inevitably follow. His spokespeople have, in turn, developed their own set of linguistic tricks to rebrand apples as oranges. They are aided by Zuma's poor use of English, for which he cannot be blamed – he is a first-language isiZulu speaker – and his vagueness, for which he can. A typical Zuma statement in response to a difficult question will say everything and nothing.

Here is an example. When the ANC National Executive Committee recalled President Thabo Mbeki, Zuma issued a statement that set out the decision but provided no cogent reason for it. In a subsequent interview, he was asked for an explanation. In response, he said the following:

> It was not how the government was doing, it was a different matter. It was different issues that related to that matter. It was never that he failed as head of government. That's why I quote him … I am saying, not that he failed to advance the programme of the ANC; there were other matters that related to government

that people had a problem with, which caused quite
serious problems in the ANC.

According to that reply, Mbeki didn't fail in government,
nor did he fail to execute the ANC's policies. Yet he was
recalled, due to 'other matters that related to government'. What these are we are never told. We only know
that 'people' had a problem with them. So, they were
widely known, but could not be articulated. And they
were a problem because they caused problems inside the
ANC in turn. How do we reconcile Mbeki's good performance as president with the fact that he was causing such
serious problems that not only did he have to be recalled,
but those problems dared not be articulated? The real
answer to that question would come one question later
in the same interview, when Zuma was asked if he would
care to elaborate. 'No, not at all,' he said.

And that is often Jacob Zuma for you – he can fill a
vacuum with empty rhetoric but, once it is all done, you
are left wondering whether he has said anything at all. It
is for this reason, too, that his off-the-cuff remarks are
often more revealing than the considered positions he
articulates.

But why does anyone care? Why is it that Jacob Zuma's
personal beliefs, values and attitudes resonate so powerfully with the media and public?

Primary among the reasons is contradiction – he is a traditional man at odds with the requirements of a modern democracy. This is perplexing for many, especially those who hold a Western set of personal values. Does Zuma really talk to the ancestors? Surely he cannot derive satisfaction from women bowing and scraping before him? Why can he not see Schabir Shaik or Nkandla for who and what they really are? People with a Western democratic mindset view Zuma through a lens entirely unsuited to the man – the Constitution. Many others see him through the very same lens as Zuma's – as a man of the people who embodies the things they believe themselves. He straddles two worlds. And he blames the media for providing a window into only one of them.

The result is that Zuma is a mass of contradictions, the epicentre from which much confusion spreads. That perplexity is doubled by his demagoguery and willingness to try to be all things to all people. Zuma might represent an inherent contradiction but he is expert at literal contradiction too.

Nothing grabs public attention like a puzzle. Many try to 'solve' the Zuma riddle, often by projecting onto him some complex, hidden sophistication that would explain away his aberrant views. It is a puzzle they will never solve, for Zuma is just being himself. No one can accuse him of being inauthentic. As with any populist, he wants to please as many people as possible. And he sees himself as an innocent victim, surrounded by individuals who do strange things in his name, of most of which he is not aware and certainly does not approve. All he wants to do, he says, is serve the ANC.

On this front, Zuma is something of an ethical black hole. He seems incapable of understanding the moral landscape. It is, to him, a maze of technical loopholes. Government itself can be perplexing, a complex bureaucratic machine that has taken on a life of its own and regularly imposes on him. He does not seem to understand that, ironically for a person who once led South Africa's moral regeneration movement, he is charged not just with implementing the principles of the Constitution but with representing the values it espouses. To Zuma, principles are regulations – they do not necessarily translate into a particular world view or set of personal convictions. Rather, they are technicalities. He is more interested in their limits than their potential. The problem is that ordinary members of the public may be at odds with the Constitution, in the privacy of their own moral universe, but not the president, whose attitudes are showcased every day.

Here the ANC is partly to blame. Zuma often articulates the party's own basic instincts. The most important quote in this book is a passing remark, made and received without a second thought way back in 1996. Back then, Zuma claimed that the ANC – and, by implication, its president – was 'more important' than the Constitution. Given this position, many other controversial Zuma statements fall into place. The ANC is the lens through which the Constitution is interpreted, not vice versa. So, it matters not who is president, or that the president is or is not intrinsically good and virtuous by his or her own standards. What matters is the fact that he or she represents the will of the ANC – which is, the party believes, the will of the people. There is no morality outside the ANC. Zuma has taken that to its ultimate conclusion by saying that the ANC is the party of God Himself.

The chapters of this book each speak to one of the recurring themes in Zuma's rhetoric. The book starts with his most basic belief system – his religious and cultural views – before moving on to the consequences of these views for his attitude to the Constitution and the rule of law. It then moves to his explanations – how he justifies his world view and his criticisms of how the media portrays his outlook. Finally, it looks at the things affected by his beliefs – his approach to power and his journey in pursuit of it, his friends and allies on that journey and the many and varied promises he made along the way. It ends with a sweeping chapter, home to those indiscretions that do not fit neatly into any of the ones it follows.

Each chapter opens with a short introduction to its theme, with quotes following chronologically. Some quotes, as is the nature of such things, apply to more than one chapter, but are placed where they are because their emphasis best illustrates the theme of the particular chapter. The quotes are referenced, in the hope that the book will itself serve as a reference and a political guide.

While every quote has a context, ultimately each stands alone as an idea or position. If anything, Jacob Zuma's greatest contribution to South Africa's democracy has been a series of debates that have forced us to examine the contradictions that run through our society. South Africa is, in many ways, a Third World democracy with First World aspirations. Zuma is often at the centre of that unfolding conflict.

Here, then, is Jacob Zuma, in his own words.

THE TEN COMMANDMENTS ACCORDING TO JACOB ZUMA

JACOB ZUMA AND RELIGION

*'People who love God must not play with their
votes; they must vote for the ANC.'*

Jacob Zuma once said, 'I start from basic Christian principles. Christianity is part of what I am; in a way it was the foundation for all my political beliefs.' That foundation, however, is not hidden underground. Often it breaks the surface to become clearly visible in his political rhetoric. He believes the ANC is divinely sanctioned by God Himself, and that a vote for the party is much more than a mere democratic right – rather, it is a supernatural moral test: the thin line between good and evil.

With that, he argues, comes consequences: those who vote for the party will find themselves in heaven, where ANC membership cards guarantee entry; those who vote against it, in hell, where the devil awaits.

This constitutes a profoundly undemocratic attitude. If politics and political parties are an extension of God's plan, then free will is denuded of its worth, as is the very purpose of elections as an extension of the will of the

3

people. The attitude is fatalistic – people can act only in a predetermined fashion, and it is the gods who are doing the determining. It is for this reason, perhaps, that he repeatedly uses the word 'rule' as opposed to 'govern'.

It is significant that many of Zuma's religious utterances are made from the electoral stump to generally uneducated, rural voters with whom religion resonates so much more powerfully. His utterances might be an authentic reflection of his personal convictions but he understands well the impact they have on the ANC's core constituency. God can be used to motivate political behaviour and augment demagogic values in equal measure much more powerfully than democratic best practice.

Supplementing all of this is a strong and long-standing bond with the church. Ordained as an honorary pastor in 2007, Zuma has visited various religious organisations repeatedly and called on them to help guide government policy and practice. Often, too, he has ensured that influential religious leaders are positioned close to him and the ANC. Not so much a separation of church and state, then, as an influential informal arrangement, whereby God and His representatives on earth are integrated into Zuma's political universe. He has not always been at peace with Christianity, which he blames for eroding traditional African values, but has no qualms about Christ, God or the Christian doctrine.

Governments should not be secular, in Zuma's opinion. They should be a vessel through which God's word is transmitted to the people. As such, they should be blessed and guided by religious authority. As the president of both the governing party and country, and a man of God himself, Zuma sees himself as ideally placed to act as the intermediary. And, as 'Africans', he argues, South Africans have a special obligation to augment this religious agenda. His influence has been pervasive, and Zuma's brand of religiosity now crops up everywhere as a result, often where it should not.

Zuma and many of his contemporaries are firmly of the belief that the ANC is blessed and, as evidence for this, they routinely point to the number of prominent religious figures who were responsible for its formation. 'When the ANC was formed, there were a lot of luminaries from the church,' said ANC Treasurer General Mathews Phosa in 2011, defending Zuma's comments that '[w]hen the ANC was born, it was baptised'. The ANC often refers to itself as a 'broad church'. That metaphor is deliberate, and appropriate on a number of different levels.

Zuma denies any comparison between himself and Christ. Many of his supporters, however, do not. On a continent where millenarianism and mysticism hold much sway, Jacob Zuma is to many as much a pastor as a president. The Bible and the Constitution guide Zuma's attitude to morality and democratic process to the same degree, and his most fervent supporters often fail to draw the proper distinction between the two, as they hang on his every word.

'We want a leader who sees poverty and walks and lives among poverty-stricken people in Nkandla,' said pastor Qiniso Shabalala, in explaining the decision to ordain Zuma in 2007. Today, Zuma no longer walks among the people of Nkandla, the ostensibly humble home from which this man of the people originates. He watches them from behind a R250 million security compound.

Solomon was well rewarded by God for choosing wisdom over wealth. Zuma, however, appears to have made a different choice.

Zuma, the ANC and God

2003

'I arrived from Jordan this morning just after 5 o'clock … I must say I took advantage of being in Jordan to go to the River Jordan where Jesus was baptised – I was around there. Jericho and Jerusalem were just across the Dead Sea. So, if I look at anyone, he or she will be blessed.' [1]

2004

'The ANC will rule South Africa until Jesus comes back.' [2]

2006

'Our client strongly rejects and distances himself from this comparison and stresses his deep-seated and sincere respect for the Christian faith.' [3]

2007

'Church leaders should be able to tell government leaders if they are straying and their laws clash with the teachings of the Lord.' [4]

---

1. Questions in the National Council of Provinces, 24 June 2003.

2. Said to a Gauteng ANC Special Council in Johannesburg. 'ANC will rule SA until Jesus comes back, says Zuma', *Business Day*, 15 March 2004.

3. From a March 2006 lawyer's letter sent on behalf of Jacob Zuma to the *Sowetan* newspaper, which, in the same month, ran an article titled '"I'm like Christ" – Zuma' in which it was claimed Zuma said he was 'like Christ' and that the media sought to 'crucify' him. Zuma claimed he was grossly misrepresented and had never made the comparison. The *Sowetan* said it stood by what it wrote. See also 'Zuma picks legal team to take on media', South African Press Association, 27 March 2006.

4. Addressing the Apostolic Faith Mission in Evaton in the Vaal Triangle. 'Challenge unchristian laws, urges Zuma', *City Press*, 8 April 2007.

'That is why we believe [the ANC] will be in power forever until the son of man comes back.'[5]

'One thing I believe history has done is to bring down the morality of people, to remove respect. People were made to have no fear; not to fear God, the Lord, and I have a view about the role religion must play ... God says that those in authority must be blessed by those who are religious, so they can govern [the] people of God accordingly. However, both in Africa and the rest of the world, very little was done by the people of God. Yes, we pray but what we do not do is participate in influencing them [the governments] to make the laws that are keeping with the values of God.'[6]

'As Africans we have to work hard so that we can have governments that fear God, therefore there will be peace, there will be democracy, respect for life.'[7]

2008

'We shall build this organisation. Even God expects us to rule this country because we are the only organisation which was

---

5. Delivering a tribute to former ANC President Oliver Tambo in Kimberley, Northern Cape, and in referring to the fact that during floor crossing 'all crossed to the ANC'. '"Ruling party is not divided"', *Diamond Fields Advertiser*, 29 October 2007.

6. An off-the-cuff speech to the African Diaspora Foundation in Los Angeles. 'Zuma delivers his views on the role of religion', *The Star*, 11 December 2007, and 'Zuma tells world his views on God', *Daily News*, 10 December 2007. ANC stalwart and member of cabinet Kader Asmal is quoted as saying in response to Zuma's comments that '[t]he constitution is the basic safeguard of our democracy. Tamper with it and you put our freedom in peril. Real leadership demands that leaders do not play to the gallery'.

7. Ibid.

blessed by pastors when it was formed.'[8]

'[The ANC] is even blessed in Heaven. That is why we will rule until Jesus comes back. We should not allow anyone to govern our city [Cape Town] when we are ruling the country.'[9]

'When all of us take office in government ... we raise our right hand and indeed pronounce ... so help me God. I believe no one can argue South Africa is not based on the principles of God.'[10]

'The bible says pray for those who are in government. I believe we must go beyond that. You must advise and criticise if there are things we do that are not in keeping with the principles of God.'[11]

2009

'It [the expression of support for the ANC] is an unequivocal biblical declaration that if God is for us, who can be against us.'[12]

---

8. Addressing more than 1 000 people at an ANC rally in Khayelitsha, Cape Town. '"ANC to rule until Jesus comes back"', *Cape Times*, 5 May 2008.

9. Ibid.

10. Addressing a National Presidential Religious Leaders summit in Kempton Park, Johannesburg. 'SA a country of God – Zuma', South African Press Association, 27 November 2008.

11. Ibid.

12. ANC press statement, 9 March 2009. The statement sets out remarks made by Jacob Zuma, then-deputy ANC president, to 'about 50 traditional leaders from various traditional houses and church leaders of diverse religions in the North West'.

'As the ANC, we're the child of the church.' [13]

'Zuma told the leaders that the ANC was the only organisation that can claim that it was baptised when it was born.' [14]

'People who love God must not play with their votes; they must vote for the ANC. We believers know that Jesus will come back; we say the ANC will rule until he comes back.' [15]

'The ANC will rule until the Son of Man comes. He must come back while we are still in power.' [16]

2011

'The ANC will rule until the guy who saved us comes back again.' [17]

'When priests pray for poverty to end and for development, then it means God agrees with the ANC because the ANC stands for those things.' [18]

'We in the ANC know God. When the ANC was born, it was baptised. We have respect, we are beautiful, we conduct ourselves in a good way.' [19]

---

13. ANC press statement, 9 March 2009.

14. Ibid. This sentiment is not a direct quote from Zuma, but attributed to him by the statement.

15. Speaking to church leaders at Kwaggafontein Stadium in Mpumalanga. 'God is on our side – Msholozi', *Sowetan*, 9 March 2009.

16. Addressing supporters in Witbank, Mpumalanga. 'ANC until "Jesus comes"', *The Times*, 22 June 2009.

17. Said at an impromptu rally at the Mthatha city hall in the Eastern Cape. 'ANC is the ticket to heaven', *Daily Dispatch*, 5 February 2011.

18. Ibid.

19. Ibid.

'When you vote for the ANC, you are also choosing to go to heaven. When you don't vote for the ANC you should know that you are choosing that man who carries a fork … who cooks people. When you are carrying an ANC membership card, you are blessed. When you get up there, there are different cards used but when you have an ANC card, you will be let through to go to heaven.' [20]

'When you get to heaven, the angels will be dressed in green, black and gold. The holy ones belong to the ANC.' [21]

'If you leave this organisation to form your own … you will struggle until you die. The ancestors of this land … Hintsa, Ngqika and Shaka will all turn their backs on you.' [22]

'Believe in two things: God and the ANC.' [23]

'When you vote for the ANC you are voting for Qamata [God], Qamata is the midst of the ANC. We are the mother of democracy, no other party deserves to be voted for other than the ANC. There's always the presence of God where we are. When you vote for the ANC even your hand gets blessed.' [24]

---

20. Said at an impromptu rally at the Mthatha city hall in the Eastern Cape. 'God is on the ANC's side, Zuma tells crowd', *Sunday Times*, 6 February 2011.

21. Ibid.

22. Ibid.

23. Said to an ANC rally in the Eastern Cape town of Graaff-Reinet on 9 April 2011, in the run-up to the local government elections. 'Vote ANC, vote God', *City Press*, 11 April 2011.

24. Ibid.

'God helps those who help themselves. He softens the hearts of government and business owners. Government is like God, quick to hear but slow to respond.'[25]

2013

'If you don't respect those in leadership, if you don't respect authority then you are bordering on a curse.'[26]

'Whether we like it or not, God has made a connection between the government and the church. That's why he says you, as a church, should pray for it.'[27]

25. Speaking to residents in Tsilitwa village, explaining a rural development programme. 'Government is like God – Zuma', *Daily Dispatch*, 21 November 2011.

26. Addressing the 33rd Presbyterian Synod in Giyani, Limpopo. 'Zuma invokes wrath of God', *The Star*, 7 October 2013.

27. Ibid.

The wisdom of Jacob's disciples

Christian religious rhetoric has, on Jacob Zuma's watch, become more prevalent both in the ANC's politicking and, perhaps more disturbingly, in the language and ideas of those representing the various arms of the state. As far as politics goes, Zuma and the ANC are regularly feted as divinely chosen to lead; with regards to the state, God himself has determined not only appointments to key positions, but government policy and programmes. From education to health, justice to democracy, increasingly God's will can be found influencing South Africa's direction and the people responsible for it.

2004

'The ANC follows the teachings of Jesus Christ. When Jesus walked the streets of Jerusalem he identified with the poor. That is what the ANC does. Jesus Christ suffered because he wanted to see people sheltered. The ANC provides Bushbuckridge with houses. Jesus Christ would have loved to see people living in healthy situations. The ANC provides clinics and food parcels. Jesus fought poverty and suffering in his preaching. The ANC provides grants to stop people from suffering. Like the Pharaohs, God did not support the Apartheid government. That is why they did not last. But God supports this government. It does what Jesus does. It will rule till Jesus comes back.'[28]

2006

'Zuma is black Jesus.'[29]

'"We like [Zuma] because he is like Jesus, he has been working hard for the freedom of the people for a long time. The indunas, the councillors, they don't deliver, but if Zuma became president then maybe he will do something for this area."'[30]

2008

'Jesus was persecuted. He was called names and betrayed. It's the same kind of suffering Mr Zuma has had to bear recently, but he's still standing strong.'[31]

---

28. From a 2004 election speech delivered by Bushbuckridge's mayor Milton Morema, just after Jacob Zuma spoke. See Niehaus, I (2006), 'Doing politics in Bushbuckridge: work, welfare and the South African elections of 2004', *Africa Journal* 76(4): 538–539.

29. One of many similar placards displayed by ANC supporters in the run-up to Jacob Zuma's 2006 rape trial and the 2007 Polokwane conference. Some would ask, 'Why are you crucifying Zuma?'; others simply stated, 'Zuma is Jesus'. See 'Zuma Jesus row', *The Citizen*, 28 March 2006.

30. Mbongeleni Biyela, a resident of Nkandla, home to Zuma's private homestead, on what Zuma would hopefully do for the area if he were to become South African president. See 'Nkandla: Our fortunes are tied to Msholozi', *Mail & Guardian*, 12 April 2006.

31. Free State ANC Chairperson Ace Magashule, explaining a similar comparison he made to a crowd of Zuma supporters outside the Supreme Court of Appeal. See 'Zuma is like Jesus, says ANC man', *Volksblad*, 30 November 2008.

2009

'In church they sing that they will follow Jesus wherever he goes. That's how we should be about Jacob Zuma.' [32]

2011

'I am one of those believers who believe that there is God and God does speak. When a position comes like this one, I wouldn't take it unless I had prayed and satisfied myself that God wants me to take it.' [33]

'The organisation [the ANC] has a responsibility to rule until Jesus pays us another visit.' [34]

2012

'As the ANC we are home to everybody and we recognise the different religious and cultural expressions. We are able to work with all these religions including African religion. There are no contradictions, because God is one, approaches to God are different, but the important thing is a goal of reaching God and the method, because the methods are manmade.' [35]

---

32. Free State ANC Chairperson Ace Magashule speaking to 900 delegates in the Bloemfontein city hall. See 'Follow Zuma "like Jesus"', *Volksblad*, 19 January 2009.

33. Chief Justice Mogoeng Mogoeng, in response to the question, 'Do you think God wants you to be appointed Chief Justice?' during his interview with the Judicial Services Commission in September 2011. Jacob Zuma would later say, on appointing Mogoeng, 'The interview was no doubt the longest, most transparent and most robust ever undertaken by a candidate of chief justice in the history of this young democracy'. See 'Mogoeng: God wants me to be chief justice', *The Times*, 4 September 2011.

34. Then-ANC Chief Whip Mathole Motshekga, to the ANC's elective conference in Polokwane, Limpopo. 'ANC must rule "until Jesus pays another visit"', *City Press*, 21 November 2011.

35. Then-ANC Chief Whip Mathole Motshekga, defending the inclusion of God and religion at the ANC's elective conference in Mangaung. 'ANC defends God's presence at Mangaung', *Sunday Independent*, 8 January 2012.

'God was acknowledged as the spiritual ruler of Mpumalanga and he was requested to rule over all of us. Leaders from government and business signed the covenant with God.'[36]

2013

'We believe nothing can defeat prayer; we will make sure that the kids are delivered from the evil spirits and believe we will get the best results this year.'[37]

'God is with the ANC and that is why we will win the 2014 general elections. As the religious leaders have pointed out, we will not fear any weapons formed against us ahead of the 2014 general elections because God is with us. We will crush anyone who contests us at these elections.'[38]

'In a discussion I once had with [former ANC President] OR Tambo, he was convinced that the ANC had its own God. That is why when you attack the party, it is you who will be destroyed. It is our responsibility to look after the children of God. This is why the people you vote for at this conference should be people who understand what should be done.'[39]

'I wish to emphasise that in the final analysis, human life is in

---

36. Pastor Johan Putter, one of the organisers of an event during which the provincial government, represented by provincial education MEC Reginah Mhaule, would sign an agreement acknowledging that 'the Christian God and the God of the Bible' was 'the spiritual leader' of the province. See 'Mpumalanga declares the Christian God the spiritual leader of province', *Mpumalanga Today*, 29 May 2012.

37. Minister of Basic Education Angie Motshekga urging Mpumalanga residents to pray for their children writing matric exams. See 'Angie Motshekga turns to prayer', *African Eye News Service*, 20 October 2013.

38. Ibid. ANC National Executive Committee member Mcebisi Skwatsha.

39. Ibid. ANC National List Committee member Sindiso Mfenyana.

the hands of God; only He has the final say and only He can declare what works and what doesn't. The rest of us are just trying our best. But beat-by-beat I believe He reveals to us, as human beings, the techniques of what works and what doesn't. I want to believe these techniques are revealed to various people among us. These people come in various styles and shapes: some will use prayer; others will use ordinary water; some will use chemicals and roots; and others will use bones and all other things human beings use in their desperation to find answers.'[40]

'The organisation is Biblical in every respect. The number three is very important, as is the number 12. Jesus had 12 disciples and in its first 100 years the ANC has had 12 presidents. We also had our own Moses. In 1993, a week after the assassination of Chris Hani, Oliver Tambo died; it was after that, in 1994, that Nelson Mandela led us through the river.'[41]

2014

'All of their plans, infused in Satanism at best, will never succeed in the future because their plans are nothing else but filled with evil.'[42]

---

40. Minister of Health Aaron Motsoaledi, responding in the National Assembly to a plea from Inkatha Freedom Party MP Mario Oriani-Ambrosini to 'establish in this country a centre that can bring together different treatments of cancer'. See Unrevised Hansard, Take 330, 22 October 2013.

41. ANC Secretary General Gwede Mantashe, to the National Union of Mineworkers in Carletonville. 'ANC-alliance is heilig, Bybels', *Beeld*, 3 November 2013. Mantashe was trying to shore up fraught inter-alliance relations.

42. Minister of Sport and Recreation Fikile Mbalula. 'Zuma booing infused in Satanism – Mbalula', South African Press Association, 6 March 2014. Mbalula had called a press conference to berate those who booed Zuma during a football match between South Africa and Brazil in Johannesburg. South Africa lost 0–5.

'It is not because of the ANC's ways that we are in government ... it is through God's will.' [43]

---

43. 'ANC in government "through God's will": Mantashe', South African Press Association, 16 March 2014. ANC Secretary General Gwede Mantashe to a church congregation in Parys in the Free State.

NO COUNTRY FOR OLD MEN

JACOB ZUMA AND AFRICAN TRADITION

'Even some Africans, who become too clever, take
a position, they become the most eloquent in
criticising themselves about their own traditions
and everything.'

In much the same way as Jacob Zuma cites his religious convictions as fundamental to his political world view, he acknowledges his traditional beliefs as primary and influential in shaping his outlook. 'My first political influence,' he says, 'was as a result of the struggles fought by traditional leaders against colonialism. I must confess upfront that both the influence of traditional and liberation struggles have played a big part in shaping the man I am today.'

These two personal forces in Zuma's life – religion and traditionalism – do not always complement each other; often they are in conflict. He blames Christianity, by way of illustration, for the decline of traditional values in African society. But any reservations he might harbour are not about the Christian doctrine itself. Rather, they are about many who advocate that faith, whom he sees as having introduced a series of Western values and practices that have done much harm to 'the African way'.

What is the African way, according to Zuma? That is a difficult question to answer definitively. Black Consciousness Movement leader Steve Biko wrote extensively about what constitutes a 'real black'; Zuma, who can claim neither Biko's intellectual clarity nor the courage of his convictions, is generally far more obscure. For Zuma, African tradition is not a philosophical world view, nor is it a cogent set of principles and values; rather, it is a kind of anecdotal wisdom. He often intersperses his rhetoric with allusions to it in an ad hoc fashion.

His private life is infused with traditional practice. Prior to the ANC's 2007 Polokwane conference, Zuma went to Impendle in KwaZulu-Natal to be 'cleansed'. It was reported that a bull was slaughtered and its head thrown into the iNzinga River, after which some 50 virgins washed their hands in the bull's blood. That is one of many such ceremonies in which he has taken part. Constantly, he seeks to appease the traditional forces that he believes exist on the other side of the mortal curtain.

That his particular interpretation of African tradition is subjective is fairly obvious. There is no single, traditional code from which he draws inspiration. Those who argue that he is misrepresenting or misunderstanding particular traditional or cultural practices round on many of the things he advocates. This is one kind of opposition.

Another kind comes from those who hold dear a set of constitutional ideals, founded on the Bill of Rights. Here the contrast between Zuma's personal traditional convictions and constitutional norms and standards is starker.

The examples are many and various. He has denounced homosexuality, although he later apologised for his remark. He sees women as subservient to men – a belief that is the consequence of a patriarchal set of values. And he believes certain practices are inherently 'black' or 'white' or 'African'.

His attitude towards women is particularly problematic. He can be deeply sexist, patronising and demeaning towards them when in traditional mode. Not only does he have in his mind a stereotype of them, as married and the bearers of children, but he believes that their 'respect' for men should be physically demonstrable.

This traditional viewpoint affects far more than his relationship with the opposite gender. He sees a definite link between race and tradition – that any black person who abandons traditional ideas in favour of some other set of values has also abandoned some genetic identity bestowed upon him or her by the ancestors themselves, if not by the colour of his or her skin. All of these positions, and many others, have caused Zuma endless trouble in the mainstream media.

He uses the overlap between tradition and religion to his political advantage, too – not only does he claim to know God's will and have the ability to interpret it for mortal men, but he is also in touch with the ancestors and able to understand and advocate their political wishes, which, conveniently, always seem to favour the ANC. South Africa is blessed, indeed, to have a series of supernatural custodians so vested in the political affairs of men, and so blindly loyal to one particular party at that.

All of these things reduce individual agency. Holding them together is a kind of subtle victimhood. For Zuma, South Africans – black South Africans, in particular – are not free agents able to discern for themselves their own identity, sexuality and political orientation, but archetypes of a generic and traditional ideal he holds, as, he would have us believe, do those supernatural beings watching over them.

Overseeing all of this is Zuma himself – a chief more than a president. He sees himself as head of the South African family, a father figure who, rather than protecting and promoting the space in which people can make choices for themselves, is there to limit that space through compliance with his traditional beliefs. He determines the patronage he is able to dispense as a result of his position by deference, political expediency and loyalty more than by any constitutional concern. Everyone – be they women, children or 'clever blacks' – has a predetermined mould into which they should be made to fit, and he is terribly disappointed when they fail to do so.

Notably, for all Zuma's traditional fundamentalism, he has had precious little to say about the darker side of African tradition – witch killings, initiation deaths and muti murders. Quick to determine which race may or may not use hair straightener, he is conveniently silent about these more deadly distortions of African cultural practice. Distortions or not, they exist, they come from somewhere and someone is responsible for them. But reflection and introspection are not part of the Zuma package. In their place is an unwritten set of values to which Zuma alone has access.

Jacob Zuma, culture and superstition

1998

'Traditional leaders are born, not elected, and cannot
be expected to do the same type of tasks as elected
representatives.'[1]

2002

'I come from the old school.'[2]

'If you as a child did something naughty and an adult from the
community saw you doing it, he could pick up a stick and beat
you. And, when your parents found out about that beating,
they would beat you again.'[3]

'[There is] far too much pornography around.'[4]

2004

'Girls knew that their virginity was their family's treasure
and boys respected that. They would only have sex when
permitted to do so by their families after marriage – something
which made them respect each other.'[5]

---

1. 'Mr peace maker', *Natal Witness*, 27 May 1998.

2. 'Tradition the key to solve social ills', *Pretoria News*, 9 April 2002.

3. Ibid.

4. Ibid.

5. Speaking at the AmaMpondomise heritage celebrations held at Emdibanisweni
   Great Place near Mthatha in the Eastern Cape, Zuma encouraged women to take
   virginity tests. He blamed previous governments for taking away the values of
   Africans under the auspices of civilisation, education and religion. See 'Zuma takes
   a stand on virginity testing', South African Press Association, 23 September 2004.

'Although virginity testing is not government policy, it is a highly prized and practised part of the culture of many of our communities. As we are faced with ever-increasing incidents of HIV and Aids, we need as a country to revitalise and restore many of our cultural traditions that could assist in the prevention of HIV and Aids.'[6]

2005

'If there are boys who are scared to propose love to girls, give them muti, so that they can have girlfriends and not go out and rape.'[7]

'Now that we are free, no religion or traditional practice should be looked down upon because other nations are practising their cultures and religions without fear in South Africa.'[8]

2006

'She then said you cannot just leave a woman at that stage, in that situation, in that position, and I said to myself I know as we grew up and in Zulu culture you do not leave a woman in that situation because if you do she may even have you arrested and say that you are a rapist.'[9]

---

6. How Zuma described virginity testing in reply to a Parliamentary question, although he stressed it should be voluntary. See 'Maagdelikheidstoetse Zuma se plan', *Beeld*, 25 November 2004.

7. Speaking at the opening of the national conference of the Traditional Health Practitioners of South Africa, at the OR Tambo municipal hall in Mthatha, Eastern Cape. 'Zuma calls on traditional healers to cleanse SA', *Daily Dispatch*, 14 October 2005.

8. Ibid. The 'other nations' Zuma cited as the Jews.

9. According to the court record, the explanation given by Zuma on 3 April for having sex with his accuser in his 2006 rape trial (*The State vs Jacob Gedleyihlekisa Zuma* 8/5/2006).

'[Same-sex marriages] are a disgrace to the nation and to
God.' [10]

'When I was growing up, an *ungqingili* [homosexual] would
not have stood in front of me. I would knock him out.' [11]

'My remarks were made in the context of the traditional
way of raising children. I commented in particular about the
manner in which communities tend to neglect the boy children
and over-emphasise the traditional upbringing of girl children
as evidenced in ceremonies such as the reed dance. I said the
communal upbringing of children in the past was able to assist
parents to notice children with a different social orientation.
I however did not intend to have this interpreted as a
condemnation of gays and lesbians ... I apologise unreservedly
for the pain and anger that my remarks may have caused.' [12]

---

10. In an address to thousands of people (including *amabutho* or warriors)
attending a Heritage Day celebration in KwaDukuza in KwaZulu-Natal on
24 September 2006. See 'On a point of clarification ... the opaque policies of
the ANC president', *Cape Times*, 31 March 2008. This quote is the primary
one attributed to Zuma on this subject but the full extent of remarks about
homosexuality is unclear from reportage on the event. For example, the
Natal Witness ('Zuma the traditionalist', 25 September 2006) – although not
directly attributing a quote to Zuma – describes his comments on the subject as
follows: 'He said there are many challenges facing the Zulu culture, including
homosexuality, which he said is something that was never condoned in the
culture and has to be guarded against'.

11. Ibid.

12. Following public outrage about his remarks on homosexuality, Zuma issued a
statement ('Statement by ANC Deputy President Jacob Zuma on remarks about
gay and lesbian community', 28 September 2006) in which he made a limited
apology.

2007

'The importance of the link of our modern society to our traditional roots must not be undermined by those of us that are very modern.' [13]

'A king is a king because of his subjects. This idiom puts people at the center of traditional governance, just as democracy is for the people by the people. Traditional and democratic systems should draw strength from each other, find common ground and not be in competition or contradiction of each other.' [14]

2010

'The problem is that people have got particular religions, values and beliefs – and people give themselves the authority to be judgmental against others and other cultures. Who gives individuals – no matter who they are – the right to be judgmental because they believe in certain cultures and values?' [15]

---

13. Addressing delegates on the closing day of the International Conference on Traditional Leadership in Durban, KwaZulu-Natal. 'Tradition survives modernity', *Natal Witness*, 27 October 2007.

14. Ibid.

15. To journalists in Cape Town following weeks of debate about his polygamous private life. See 'Zuma – "Issues nothing to do with debate"', *The Times*, 24 February 2010.

2011

'We have passed laws that prohibit you as a parent [from using] corporal punishment. Today, when, as a parent, you bring your child [to] order by using corporal punishment, you are breaking the law, but the person who passed that law cannot raise your child the way you want to.' [16]

'As Africans, long before the arrival of religion and [the] gospel, we had our own ways of doing things ... Those were times that the religious people refer to as dark days, but we know that, during those times, there were no orphans or old age homes. Christianity has brought along these things.' [17]

2012

'The continued display of the portrait is a grave violation of my right to dignity as it depicts me with my private parts showing.' [18]

'I was happy because I wouldn't want to stay with daughters who are not getting married. Because that in itself is a problem

---

16. Speaking at KwaMaphumulo, on the KwaZulu-Natal north coast, during the launch of a road safety and crime awareness campaign. See 'Now for the gospel according to Zuma', *The Times*, 21 December 2011.

17. Ibid.

18. Founding Affidavit for Mr JG Zuma in the matter between Jacob Gedleyihlekisa Zuma (First Applicant), African National Congress (Second Applicant); and Goodman Gallery (First Respondent), *City Press* (Second Respondent), in the Gauteng South High Court. Case number: 17978/2012. Brett Murray's painting *The Spear* did much to evoke an intense reaction from Zuma and the ANC. Much of this reaction was fuelled by the idea that Zuma, as South Africa's president, should be immune from satire and ridicule. The idea was that he should be respected (that is, not mocked) as a result of his station. That impulse is largely based on a traditional understanding of respect – something demanded, not earned. It flows from a belief that high office, much like that of a chief or king, necessitates deference.

in society. People today think being single is nice. It's actually not right. That's a distortion. You've got to have kids. Kids are important to a woman because they give extra training to a woman, to be a mother.' [19]

'Even some Africans, who become too clever, take a position, they become the most eloquent in criticising themselves about their own traditions and everything.' [20]

'Even if you apply any kind of lotion and straighten your hair you will never be white.' [21]

'[People who love dogs more than humans suffer] a lack of humanity.' [22]

---

19. Excerpt from an interview with Dali Tambo, on his programme *People of the South*, SABC 3, 19 August 2012.

20. Speech to the National House of Traditional Leaders in Parliament, 1 November 2012. This quote, repackaged in different wording by many on social media and in the mainstream press, has become commonly referred to as Zuma's 'clever blacks' remark.

21. Speaking at the annual commemoration of the induction of Inkosi Sibongiseni Zuma at Impendle in KwaZulu-Natal. See 'Pet dogs not for blacks – Zuma', *The Mercury*, 27 December 2012.

22. Ibid. It is a curious fact that, despite the uproar that Zuma's comments about having a pet generated, there exists no direct quote ever attributed to him. The story in *The Mercury*, which broke the news of his comments, opens with the following, which was later attributed to Zuma as a direct quote by many other newspapers, but which, in the original story, appears only as a paraphrase of his remarks: 'Spending money on buying a dog, taking it to the vet and for walks belonged to white culture and was not the African way, which was to focus on the family, President Jacob Zuma said in a speech in KwaZulu-Natal on Wednesday.' In defending the remarks later, however, the Presidency confirmed that Zuma did express such a sentiment.

'A national cleansing ceremony.'[23]

2013

'When I was in Venda recently I was so impressed to see how people there express respect for other people. A woman would clap her hands and even lie down to show respect. I was so impressed. If I was not already married to my wives I would go to Venda to look for a woman.'[24]

23. Speaking at a traditional cleansing ceremony in KwaZulu-Natal, in his capacity as president. 'Zuma calls for a national cleansing ceremony', SABC News, 28 December 2012. Zuma would say, in explaining his motivation, that '[w]e have a problem that respect for life has almost come to zero, just respect of other person, respect of the leaders, respect of organisations, whatever the call, but respect of life that people today find it's very easy to kill another person'. Zuma stated that he would call on Archbishop Emeritus Desmond Tutu to lead the ceremony, but nothing ever came of it, no doubt because the state has no business imposing religious practices onto its citizens.

24. Addressing hundreds of people at Impendle, KwaZulu-Natal. See 'Zuma's Venda women comments slammed', *The Mercury*, 20 December 2013.

ZUMBABWE

JACOB ZUMA ON ROBERT MUGABE AND ZIMBABWE

'And I can tell you, nobody in the world can say they have done better on Zimbabwe than us.'

If Jacob Zuma believes himself to be a South African father figure, then Robert Mugabe is the African patriarch he appears to aspire to become. And the impulse of appreciation for Mugabe has always been demagogic in nature: 'The people love him. So how can we condemn him?' he asked in hand-wringing fashion in 2006.

This is not an attitude unique to Zuma. The ANC in general and much of its support base has held Mugabe in high esteem since he was first elected to power. But in Zuma, first as deputy president and later as president, the South African government had a front-line spokesperson for its policy of quiet diplomacy and general appeasement as Mugabe systematically rode roughshod over democratic best practice in a once-flourishing new African democracy.

Many of Zuma's statements about Zimbabwe can thus be found in the archives of the National Assembly where, as deputy president, he would routinely defend then-President Thabo Mbeki and the lack of decisive or principled action by the South African government against the tyranny of Mugabe's ZANU–PF. The standard defence was that Zimbabwe was a sovereign country and South Africa was constrained in the degree to which it could influence the slow-motion implosion across the Limpopo River. In truth, the options available to the South African government, essentially an economic life-support system for the Zimbabwean economy, were many and far-ranging. But these were not enacted with any sense of purpose, if they were enacted at all.

When Zuma was not defending the indefensible, he was embracing it. He was among the first to endorse the sto-len 2002 presidential election as free and fair, and was seen shaking hands with and hugging Mugabe as the results were confirmed. It was at about this time that his defence of quiet diplomacy peaked; the record is loaded with his explanations for it. Formally, he would defend a limited approach in Parliament, suggesting a problem but pleading diplomatic constraint; informally, he would smile and embrace a demagogic tyrant with salutations and congratulations.

Zuma's defence of Mbeki is revealing. In much the same way as he would use Parliament to defend the former president's controversial position on HIV/Aids, Zuma would often take to the podium to stand up for a softly spoken government. As president, Zuma abandoned Mbeki's Aids quackery – although he was careful never to denounce Mbeki for it – but on Zimbabwe he has overseen a fairly seamless transition. To this day, Zimbabwe is shielded from proper criticism by Zuma's administration, which cowers before Mugabe – much as Mbeki did before.

The parallels suggest that, while Zuma and Mbeki fell out over many issues, reinforcing both leaders were nationalistic impulses that demanded solidarity with the political parties that helped the ANC during the struggle – parties that, on the basis of racial solidarity, reflected the ANC's attitude to the national democratic revolution and the fight against what Mugabe often terms Western imperialism. In many respects, Robert Mugabe presents a less restrained version of some of the impulses that underpin the ANC's agenda.

Zimbabwe has also been a convenient political tool in Zuma's hands. After defending quiet diplomacy for years in Parliament as deputy president (during which time he had said that it was 'not the duty of this country' to 'correct, run and monitor presidents of other countries'), as soon as Zuma had a chance of being elected president, he changed his tune, albeit temporarily. Thus, there was a fleeting period in which Zuma seemed to find his moral conscience. His party position secured at Polokwane and unencumbered by the weight of the South African presidency, from 2007 to 2009 he would occasionally allude to the fact that Mugabe had overstayed his welcome. But it was only ever populist posturing, something he did much of during that period.

As soon as he was elected president, his moral clarity seemed, once again, to blur. The government's position on Zimbabwe under Jacob Zuma remains defined by hushed whispers and more public endorsement than condemnation. At the conclusion of the 2013 Zimbabwean national elections, and in the face of significant international concern over their validity, Zuma would offer President Mugabe his 'profound congratulations' – an apt summary of his general attitude to the subject.

Jacob Zuma on Zimbabwe

2000

'[I]t is not in my nature to correct, run and monitor presidents of other countries. It is not the duty of this country to do so.' [1]

'If South Africa were to comment on every other president in the world, I am sure we would be a mad country.' [2]

2002

'This election was legitimate, valid, free and fair.' [3]

'We sent observers here, who were observing each and every detail. They have reported ... the elections were legitimate, are valid. They were free and fair and we have got to respect that.' [4]

---

1. Answering questions in the National Assembly. Hansard, 1 November 2000, p. 4334.

2. Ibid.

3. Said in an interview with the Zimbabwe Broadcasting Corporation (ZBC) television about the 2002 Zimbabwean presidential elections. Sent to Zimbabwe as President Mbeki's emissary, Zuma delivered a message of congratulations to Mugabe from the South African president. Zuma said his country shared the views of other African organisations, such as the Organization of African Unity (OAU) and the Southern African Development Community (SADC), whose observers 'were here' and who 'did not get information from the media'. "Those discrediting Zimbabwe's electoral process should listen to what the Africans are saying', Zuma told the interviewer. 'Amandla!'" See 'Summit in London to weigh Zimbabwe's suspension from Commonwealth', Sapa-AFP; 15 March 2002.

4. Said with President Robert Mugabe, after hugging and exchanging clenched-fist salutes. See 'South African deputy hails Mugabe victory', *Daily Telegraph*, 15 March 2002. The newspaper also stated that British officials had admitted that 'what mattered to Mr Mugabe was South Africa's position. Mr Zuma's endorsement would have delighted him.'

'[W]hat the [South African] Government cannot do is to take
any action without discussing it with the government of
Zimbabwe. I do not think that there is any government that
can go to any country and start interacting with its people
without discussing it with their government. That is why we
have been saying that we are engaging the government in
Zimbabwe on this matter. And, if agreed, we will certainly
go along with involving whoever needs to be involved in
Zimbabwe to address the problem. There is absolutely no
problem with that.'[5]

'We have said that we are involved in quiet diplomacy. We have
never said we are not involved.'[6]

'The hon member has a problem, a very serious and arrogant
problem of thinking that one can move from one country and
run the affairs of other countries. That is very arrogant. The
South African Government cannot go to some country and
say: why are you mistreating this particular farmer? Where has
the hon member ever heard that? He can say that if he is not
running any country. He has no responsibility and that cannot
happen.'[7]

---

5. Answering questions in the National Assembly. Hansard, 8 May 2002, p. 857.

6. Answering questions in the National Assembly. Hansard, 11 September 2002,
   pp. 3272–3276. The quotes that follow (notes 7–11) constitute a collection of
   responses to a series of back-to-back questions, and do not represent a single
   speech. They also represent another defence of quiet diplomacy, this time in the
   face of the rigged 2002 Zimbabwean presidential elections. It makes for ironic
   reading in the light of some of Zuma's later pronouncements but, significantly, it
   is also internally inconsistent. For example, Zuma starts by saying that no country
   should comment on the affairs of other countries; then, presented with evidence
   of other countries doing exactly that, he says South Africa doesn't do that.

7. Ibid.

'[A]gain, we have a problem because the hon member wants us to emulate France and Germany. We cannot do that. We cannot do that. We are South Africa and we will remain South Africa, with our clear policies on how to relate to other countries. We cannot be told by other countries what to do, and what not to do.'[8]

'I can tell the hon member that if, one day, any country tries to suggest how South Africa must run its affairs, we would have a serious problem with that country. We cannot do that. That is very clear. We cannot help that hon member. We cannot go to Zimbabwe and tell Zimbabweans to do this and not do that. That is not our duty. That is not what we were elected to do. We were elected to run South Africa not Zimbabwe.'[9]

'South Africa has done something that other countries have not done: it has engaged the Zimbabwean government in quiet diplomacy. The [African Charter on Human and People's Rights] guides us on how we should handle our affairs in the continent. I am sure that it should be left to the country that will take action to reach a point where it feels it is necessary to take that particular action with regards to that charter.'[10]

'If South Africa has not reached that point and if it is engaging Zimbabwe, and if it has not come to the point that it should do that, why should it do it? There is no reason why we can do it when we are not convinced we have reached that time. As I

---

8. Hansard, 11 September 2002, pp. 3272–3276.

9. Ibid.

10. Ibid.

say, we have been engaging Zimbabwe and we have not come
to a point where we have to look at that charter. We think that
the manner in which we are dealing with Zimbabwe, at the
moment, is sufficient.' [11]

'We cannot say that if there is a country that does things
that other people are not happy about it must be dealt with.
Actually, I am not certain why we always want Zimbabwe
to be punished even before the rules are in place.' [12]

'If I were to ask a question, it would be: What is it about
Zimbabwe that makes everybody feel so agitated? I do not
know. Let us deal with the matters without mentioning
Zimbabwe, and mention Zimbabwe when it is necessary. One
will find that hon members just want to mention Zimbabwe as
if there is somebody keeping score somewhere on how many
times Zimbabwe is mentioned. Why?' [13]

2003

'Zimbabwe will not influence the developments in South
Africa. Why not? Because it will not.' [14]

---

11. Hansard, 11 September 2002, pp. 3272–3276.

12. Answering questions in the National Assembly. Hansard, 13 November 2002,
    p. 5036. Another defence of silent diplomacy and Robert Mugabe's rule at the
    expense of democratic principles and values. It is also evidence of another
    ANC trait – feigning ignorance in the face of a crisis.

13. Ibid.

14. Answering questions in the National Assembly, in response to a question about
    whether the situation in Zimbabwe would have any repercussions for South
    Africa's hosting of the Cricket World Cup. It did, of course, have repercussions –
    both England and New Zealand refused to play there. Hansard, 21 May 2003,
    p. 1919.

2004

'With regard to the point you zoomed on in [*sic*], Zimbabwe, I don't think South Africa could do more than what it is doing in terms of engaging Zimbabweans to discuss the issues that affect Zimbabwe and which, in the final analysis, will have to be resolved by the Zimbabweans.' [15]

'We have sought to engage both the Zimbabwean government and the opposition to discuss the issues as we see them and to hear how they feel about them. We believe that progress has been made in that direction. So, insofar as Zimbabwe is concerned, we are certain that perceptions will be dealt with or addressed very soon.' [16]

2005

'Our approach now is focused on assisting Zimbabwe to realise its own express commitment to the SADC guidelines.' [17]

'We are not in the business of condemning countries because it is not our business to run other countries.' [18]

---

15. Answering questions in the National Assembly, during the run-up to South Africa's 2004 general election. Hansard, 25 February 2004, p. 117.

16. Ibid.

17. Answering questions in the National Assembly, with regards to the 2005 Zimbabwean elections, also widely condemned as flawed. Perhaps the biggest problem with Zuma's view, its obvious bias aside, is that it completely ignores the series of rigged elections that preceded the 2005 election. The sudden and late inflation of the votes for President Robert Mugabe remains unexplained to this day. Hansard, 2 March 2005, pp. 54–57.

18. Ibid.

'In line with the Zimbabwean commitment to conduct the
coming elections free and fair, the Zimbabwean government
has invited South Africa to come and observe the elections
in five capacities: As part of SADC, as chair of the organ on
politics, defence and security, as a neighbouring country of
Zimbabwe, as the ANC and as part of the parliamentary forum.
This parliament has taken a decision about it. This clearly is
an intention of a country that is preparing to have free and
fair elections, that wants its neighbours and everybody else to
come and observe. I do not know why we should be talking
about the elections, that they are not free and fair when they
have not happened. I do not know. I absolutely do not know.' [19]

'I really do not know why we think there is going to be such
problems in Zimbabwe. In Iraq almost yesterday there were
bomb attacks and people died. There was a high incidence
of violence as the elections were going on and I never heard
the noises that I am now hearing here. Why on Zimbabwe
in particular? The hon member is telling me a fairy tale. We
must now sit and plan the strategy on what will happen after
the elections if there is a problem. We must actually spend
resources because we have in our minds that, because this is
Zimbabwe, there is going to be a crisis after the election. Why
are we prejudging Zimbabwe? How do I answer a question that
says: What are the strategies if the economy, etc.? Really, I do
not want to tell a fairy tale.' [20]

---

19. Hansard, 2 March 2005, pp. 54–57.
20. Ibid.

2006

'The Europeans often ignore the fact that Mugabe is very popular among Africans. In their eyes, he has given blacks their country back after centuries of colonialism.' [21]

'The people love him. So how can we condemn him? Many in Africa believe that there is a racist aspect to European and American criticism of Mugabe. Millions of blacks died in Angola, the Republic of Congo and Rwanda. A few whites lost their lives in Zimbabwe, unfortunately, and already the West is bent out of shape.' [22]

2007

'It is even more tragic that other world leaders who witness the repression [in Zimbabwe] pretend that it is not happening or is exaggerated. When history eventually deals with the dictators, those who stood by and watched the deterioration of nations should bear the consequences.' [23]

2008

'The policy of the ANC is what we have done in Zimbabwe. Because what has been done in Zimbabwe, many people think it was just Mbeki, but we discussed the matters about

---

21. In an interview with the German magazine *Der Spiegel.* '"The West is bent out of shape"', *Der Spiegel,* 20 December 2006. Said in response to the following: '… Pretoria continues to exercise great restraint when it comes to Robert Mugabe, who has turned neighboring Zimbabwe into a dictatorship and has forced whites from their land and driven them out of the country'.

22. Ibid. Said in response to the following: 'Mugabe has grown into a dictator, and his country is isolated internationally and economically in ruins. It has more than 1,000 percent inflation'.

23. 'Zuma puts the knife in Mbeki', *The Citizen,* 11 December 2007. In a speech at The University of the Witwatersrand on the government's policy of quiet diplomacy and Mugabe's human rights violations.

Zimbabwe and he was implementing what the ANC had decided we needed to do. And I can tell you, nobody in the world can say they have done better on Zimbabwe than us. Because nobody can produce any report of any significance as to what it is they have done to help Zimbabwe out of the problem. Some will tell you they've applied sanctions – have they helped? Some will say, we have condemned him – has it helped? We engaged with Zimbabweans, partly precisely because of that concern that we knew that to us, the Zimbabwean issue was not remote.' [24]

'I don't think so.' [25]

'What else has worked in Zimbabwe? If you single out quiet diplomacy, what else has worked? There is nothing that has worked. So it can't be fair to criticise silent diplomacy and not criticise everything else that has not worked.' [26]

'It has been worse all the time. People exaggerate Zimbabwe. I am one person who looks at things as they are.' [27]

2010

24. 'Jacob Zuma interview', *Financial Times*, 6 March 2008. Confirmation that silent diplomacy was not President Mbeki's initiative (although he may have been its biggest proponent); the ANC as a whole was responsible for it. Remember, of course, that, at the time of this interview, Zuma had been elected ANC president.

25. 'Mbeki to meet Mugabe, Zuma doubts fair vote', *Reuters* , 18 June 2008. In response to the question, 'Do you think the elections in Zimbabwe will be free and fair?' Zuma said elsewhere, 'I think we'll be lucky if we have a free election.'

26. 'No racism in South Africa', *Sunday Vision*, 20 July 2008. In an interview with the Ugandan newspaper, Zuma was reportedly visibly irritated with the question about whether quiet diplomacy had worked.

27. Ibid.

'On Zimbabwe, we gave leadership before anybody else did
and the current power-sharing deal was facilitated by South
Africa.'[28]

2012

'I wouldn't because in Zimbabwe Zanu-PF holds its conferences,
they elect Mugabe; I don't look at how that happened. They
regularly hold elections and that's why you could say these
elections did not go very well. What else do you need? People
do things in different places in different ways.'[29]

'It's good. We were freedom fighters together, we know each
other from way back. So I've known him for a long time.'[30]

2013

'H E President Jacob Zuma extends his profound congratulations to H E President Robert G Mugabe on his re-election as
President of the Republic of Zimbabwe following the success-
ful harmonised elections held on 31 July 2013. President Zuma
urges all political parties in Zimbabwe to accept the outcome
of the elections as election observers reported it to be an
expression of the will of the people.'[31]

---

28. 'Lifting sanctions will give Zim a chance, says Zuma', South African Press
    Association, 29 September 2010.

29. 'Jacob Zuma denies rift with Mugabe: "We were freedom fighters together"',
    The Guardian, 12 December 2012. In response to the suggestion that Robert
    Mugabe was a dictator.

30. Ibid. Julius Malema had suggested that Zuma hated Mugabe. This was Zuma's
    response when that was put to him.

31. 'Media Statement: President Jacob Zuma congratulates President Robert Mugabe',
    4 August 2013. On the outcome of the 2013 Zimbabwean national elections.
    Mugabe was re-elected president for a seventh term and his party, Zanu-PF, won a
    two-thirds majority.

JACOB ZUMA VERSUS THE CONSTITUTION

ZUMA, THE ANC, THE CONSTITUTION AND THE RULE OF LAW

'You have fewer rights because you are a minority.'

The epicentre of the conflict between Jacob Zuma's private convictions and his public duties as the primary custodian of South Africa's democratic principles and values is the Constitution. He enjoys a love-hate relationship with it. The same applies to the rule of law. For Zuma, the ANC sits atop South Africa's legal and moral framework – everything else falls below, with the Constitution merely formalising that relationship. He is very good at explaining this belief from the top down. From the bottom up, however, he struggles badly. This is disturbing because, in truth, the natural order of things places the Constitution and the Bill of Rights above all else.

Zuma evokes laws and regulations to the finest technical detail to maximise the privileges that his high office affords – from public money spent on upgrading his personal residence in Nkandla to using state coffers to defend himself in court against the many criminal charges brought against him. Yet, conveniently, he seems able to divorce them from any ethical considerations he and others in the ANC might have about how they are applied.

At the other end of the spectrum, Zuma demonstrates great difficultly in placing the Constitution at the apex of South Africa's democratic order. It is, in his patriarchal universe, 'the daughter of the ANC'; thus, the ANC remains primarily responsible for South Africa's founding set of values and principles. Perhaps more significantly, he believes that his party is the political lens through which the Constitution should be viewed, not vice versa. The ANC, he believes, is 'more important' than the Constitution.

The result is that key constitutional tenets – the right to life, bail and a fair trial, the need for guilt to be proven beyond reasonable doubt, minority rights – have all been subjected to Zuma's demagoguery at some point or other. If the ANC represents the will of the people, right and wrong can all be put to the popular vote. Pragmatism, not principle, rules the roost.

The judiciary is, in turn, a source of great frustration for Zuma. It routinely finds against his government, its laws and its conduct, which he believes to be a kind of political advocacy on the part of the courts that often over-extend themselves to uphold the Constitution. For

Zuma, whether a particular policy contravenes the Bill of Rights is neither here nor there – it comes from the ANC, from the people, and therefore constitutes a more authentic expression of the democratic will than any court could ever muster.

A long-time sufferer at the hands of lawyers, he seems to reserve a particular contempt for them. He sees them as cold and detached and, in applying their trade, removing the human element from the legal system. The result, he argues, is the abandonment of a people-centred, 'African' approach to justice and a system that cares little for the feelings of the individuals it processes.

There is truth in what Zuma says, but much of his criticism is born of his own experience, and thus tainted by resentment. If it were not, he would place greater emphasis on restoring the criminal justice system to a place of pride. The majority of its problems, certainly the desperately slow rate at which its wheels turn, are due to severe underfunding – a condition further exacerbated by the increased politicisation of key posts both on the bench and in the prosecuting authority, all in the name of demographic representation and increased control.

All of the quotes that follow speak to this conflict, which runs like a fault line through Zuma's interactions with the criminal justice system. Always, he asks, What is the relationship between the ANC and the law? And always, his answer is that the ANC is paramount.

The result is a subversion of democratic best practice. Instead of the ANC (like every other citizen and organisation) being accountable to the Constitution and, with it, the people, it is accountable only to its own leadership and, to a lesser extent, its members. When Zuma isn't subverting this relationship, particularly through his defence of the ANC's policy of cadre deployment (the placing of party loyalists into public positions designed to be neutral, to deliver control to the party), he is blurring the line between party and state.

Jacob Zuma, freedom and justice

1996

'There is no Premier who is a Premier out of nowhere. They are all coming from the political party. They are answerable and accountable to the party, including the President and everybody else. The President of this country is the President of the ANC. No one person can be above the ANC. He can't be.'[1]

'Once you begin to feel you are above the ANC, you are in trouble ...'

'[The ANC is] more important [than the Constitution]'

'No political force can destroy the ANC – it is only the ANC that can destroy itself ...'

'[The Constitution is only there] to regulate matters.'[2]

---

1. Interview with Padraig O'Malley, in response to the question about the ANC's decision to remove Mosiuoa Lekota as Free State premier. In 1996, Jacob Zuma served the ANC as its national chairperson. The party was experiencing considerable internal turmoil in the Free State, which revolved, by and large, around Premier Mosiuoa 'Terror' Lekota. (Lekota had exercised his constitutional right to fire an MEC without consulting the ANC National Executive Committee [NEC]. As a result, the NEC removed him from office.) The Heart of Hope, available online at http://www.nelsonmandela.org/omalley/index.php/site/q/03lv00017/04lv00344/05lv00965/06lv01075.htm, 12 November 1996.

2. Addressing delegates at an ANC regional meeting in Durban, KwaZulu-Natal, explaining the decision to remove Mosiuoa Lekota as Free State premier. Zuma was called in to resolve the dispute. His primary goal was to re-enforce the ANC's policy of cadre deployment and, with it, the principle that party members were accountable first and foremost to the ANC. 'Zuma warns ANC leaders', *Eastern Province Herald*, 18 November 1996; and 'Don't lose touch with grassroots', *Natal Witness*, 18 November 1996.

1997

'These animals should not enjoy the same rights as every other SA citizen. There should be no bail for them and the punishment they get needs upgrading.'[3]

2001

'The ANC-led government distinguishes between party work and government work. The hon member is aware that this is the first time in this country that we have witnessed such a distinct separation of state interests and the interests of the ruling party.'[4]

'No party would be able to abuse its power, because the constitution and these institutions are there as watchdogs in order to ensure that nothing goes wrong.'[5]

---

3. 'Staying out of the election bun-fight', *Pretoria News*, 3 November 1997. On rapists. This profoundly unconstitutional suggestion is worth elaborating on. Section 35 (3) (h) of the South African Bill of Rights states that every accused person has a right to a fair trial, which includes the right 'to be presumed innocent'. And section 35 (1) (f) states that every person arrested for an alleged crime has the right 'to be released from detention if the interests of justice permit, subject to reasonable conditions'. Were this not the case – were the charge of rape enough to arrest and hold an accused person for trial – the door to false accusation and a fundamental abuse of the criminal justice system would be opened. Anyone could lay a charge of rape against any other person and, on that basis alone, the accused could be imprisoned (in South Africa, with a desperately under-resourced court system, no doubt for a substantial period of time) ahead of a trial to determine their guilt or innocence. As things stand, if there exists powerful circumstantial evidence, a court can deny bail, but the state needs to make that case, in order to overcome the first principle right that everyone is assumed innocent until proven guilty.

4. Answering questions in the National Assembly about the ANC's policy of cadre deployment, in which party members are deployed to key positions of power, to deliver control of the state to the ANC. Hansard, 13 June 2001, pp. 2253–2256. These responses (in notes 5 and 6) are to a series of different questions, which all relate to a central question, and thus do not constitute a single, consistent speech.

5. Ibid.

'No, having a member who serves in the Government and who also belongs to the structures of the party does not retard this particular objective [the separation of party and state]. It does not.'[6]

2002

'They [lawyers] are paid millions by the crooks to get them out of jail and that is all they are interested in. [They are] not interested in promoting good values in society. Every criminal you see behind bars these days has a pocket copy of the Constitution, he knows all his rights.'[7]

'[Judges should convict] even if there are facts that are short.'[8]

'One cannot say, when [a person] does not have the majority that the ANC has, that he needs the same voting power. That is not democratic. When the ANC says blue, it says blue. That is democracy and it is voting … It is the majority view being heard clearly. When the member says red and we do not hear it, it is not our problem. This is democracy in practice.'[9]

6. Hansard, 13 June 2001, pp. 2253–2256.

7. 'If we look to our roots we will find what we need to shape our future', *Saturday Star*, 6 April 2002. As head of the government's moral regeneration movement, Zuma gave a number of interviews advocating high moral standards. The two quotes from the same interview (see also note 8), although edited differently for different publications, perhaps exemplify Zuma's contradictory relationship with lawyers. On one hand, he resents them; on the other, he has been happy to spend millions of rands of public money for his various legal defences, exploiting every loophole and technicality to waylay a trial. Zuma is, in many ways, the biggest beneficiary of the kind of legal bureaucracy he claims to despise.

8. 'Zuma aims to rebuild pride in who we are', *Pretoria News*, 9 April 2002. This is a remarkable sentiment, drawn from the same interview as the one cited in note 7 above but edited differently for the *Pretoria News*. A remarkable position for a man who, at one stage, faced over 700 charges himself. The idea that one should prosecute a person even when the evidence is incomplete is the very antithesis of the principle that all are equal before the law and constitutionally entitled to a fair trial.

9. Answering questions in the National Assembly. Hansard, 13 November 2002, pp. 5050–5052. Here, Zuma answers a question from the African Christian Democratic Party (ACDP) about the fact that minority parties get very little speaking time in Parliament.

2003

'Therefore the answer is no. The law and government policy
on the matter are very clear … There are many issues on
which we could call referendums. I don't know where
we would end … I think we should exercise a measure of
some responsibility … no, I don't think they will accept a
referendum on any of the issues. The raising of this issue
is very selective and is done deliberately for political
convenience. But it also fails to acknowledge is the morality
of all of us towards respect for life, something which we
respect. That is why I have said that if there were specific
issues that we are not dealing with responsibly, we could
actually turn this country into a banana republic, because
there are so many people who are not satisfied with certain
things. So we have to exercise responsible government in
order to lead this country properly.' [10]

2004

'If you are a government official, how can you say: Today I am
not a government official and so you resign from your position
so that you can campaign? How do you distinguish these two?
How do you say that because I am a Minister, well, let me not
campaign because some are going to say that I am abusing
my position. It's [sic] can't be. You have to campaign for your
party. The fact that you are a Minister is just hard luck. You are
a Minister because you are elected into a position, just as your

10. Answering questions in the National Assembly. Hansard, 13 November 2003,
pp. 4345–4346. One of Zuma's more fundamental contradictions is his about-turn
on the possibility of a referendum on the death penalty, when compared with his
later (2008) position. The Constitution outlawed the death penalty as a violation
of the right to life.

party was elected by the people of this country.'[11]

2006

'I wanted to be three things – a teacher, priest or lawyer. I realise now that I should have been a lawyer because of my belief in justice.'[12]

'There are those who don't know that and think that other things are more important than the ANC. If you are not loyal to the ANC, you can't be loyal to anything else, even the Constitution. If the ANC gets weak, there will be no South Africa.'
'How can a person live, if not for the ANC?'[13]

2008

'The fact of the matter is that we don't have that penalty in the country. It was abolished by the Constitutional Court, right, for very good, cogent argument. But there are people who argue that, whilst nobody has a right to take anybody's life, criminals do. What do you do with them? And they say, well bring the death penalty. The point I was making was that, if people make that call, we can't stop them, we can't say, look, even if the overwhelming feeling is that we need a referendum for

---

11. Answering questions in the National Assembly. Hansard, 25 February 2004, p. 36. Responding to a question about the government's Ten Years of Freedom campaign, which conveniently conflated the ANC and the government.

12. 'I'm like Christ – Zuma', *Sowetan*, 24 March 2006.

13. Speaking to a gathering of ANC supporters in the Eastern Cape. In the same speech, Zuma reminded the crowd about his intervention in 1996 when he stated that the ANC was 'more important' than the Constitution. 'Grondwet is nie wapen', *Beeld*, 29 November 2006.

an example, because that's the only thing you could do. And
I said, yesterday, if they say we want a referendum, we can't
stop them. Because we are a democratic country. We can't
suppress other people's views, because we feel another way.
I say, if there is sufficient majority that says so, we should have
a referendum on the matter. Because crime is there, the crime
is there and is a problem. And some of the people who say
this, they are not saying it from a theoretical point of view,
it's because they feel some have been directly affected.' [14]

'How do you stop crime? Maybe we should think about
scrapping bail for specific crimes such as rape, killing,
and robbery. Shouldn't we discuss this in the process [of
strengthening] the fight against crime?' [15]

2009

'The point I was making was that if there was medical
evidence for him to go on parole, why would I not? Because
I would do that for anyone because that is within the law.' [16]

'There is nothing in the Constitution that says a massive
majority for the ruling party is bad for democracy, especially

14. 'Jacob Zuma interview', *Financial Mail*, 6 March 2008. This is a complete
    about-turn on his 2003 position on the subject of the death penalty. The call for a
    referendum had gone from a 'political convenience' to a democratic right. He has
    never acted on this promise.

15. Speaking to an audience of some 3 000 who attended an ANC *imbizo* on the
    University of Pretoria's Vista campus. 'Zuma suggests scrapping bail for rape
    and murder', *Cape Times*, 19 May 2008. Perhaps the ultimate populist call of any
    demagogue is the call to scrap bail, a profoundly unjust idea that runs contrary to
    the principle of innocence until proven guilty.

16. Denying claims that he promised to parole Schabir Shaik if he became president.
    The president did, however, parole Shaik, on the grounds that he suffered
    from a life-threatening illness. 'JZ defends Shaik', *Independent on Saturday*,
    14 March 2009.

a party that has a track record of upholding the Constitution like the ANC.' [17]

'The government is the daughter of the ANC.' [18]

2010

'Why should I pardon him when he hasn't applied? I have nothing in front of me. If there was an application before me, you should ask the question. Why should I respond if I do not have the application before me?' [19]

'Whether a person is fit or proper to be entrusted with the responsibilities of the office concerned is my subjective decision. I am the person, as the president of the Republic, to be satisfied that the person is fit and proper. In doing so I have to take cognisance of his/her experience, conscientiousness and integrity.' [20]

17. 'Nothing wrong with majority', *Sowetan*, 20 April 2009.

18. Addressing supporters in Witbank, Mpumalanga. 'ANC until "Jesus comes"', *The Times*, 22 June 2009.

19. In a television interview, on speculation that he was considering pardoning convicted felon Schabir Shaik. eTV, 11 January 2010. Zuma's comment, however, contradicted a 19 October 2009 letter from the Presidency, confirming that Shaik had applied for pardon. It stated: 'The Presidency received an application for pardon from Mr Schabir Shaik last year, on 24 April 2008'. Shaik was granted medical parole in 2009.

20. Answering Affidavit for President JG Zuma in the North Gauteng High Court. Case number: 59628109. In the matter between the Democratic Alliance and the President of the Republic and others, 21 May 2010. This was the crux of Zuma's defence of his decision to appoint Advocate Menzi Simelane as the director of public prosecutions. The court disagreed. Although the High Court found in favour of Zuma, the Supreme Court of Appeals would overturn that decision in finding Simelane was not, in fact, fit and proper for the position.

2012

'Sorry, we have more rights here because we are a majority. You have fewer rights because you are a minority. Absolutely, that's how democracy works. So, it is a question of accepting the rules within democracy and you must operate in them.' [21]

'I said, one day, Africans are different. During our time we did not have prisons because never did we say there was a problem could not be resolved. No problem could not be resolved. Every problem can be resolved. Prisons are done by people who cannot resolve problems.' [22]

'Let us not be influenced by other cultures and try to think that lawyers are going to help us. Because lawyers will never change facts, no matter what the judge says. I always criticize legal people, I know there are many lawyers here. For they will tell you "we are dealing with cold facts". What they don't tell you is that these cold facts deal with warm bodies ... Let us solve African problems the African way, not the white man's way.' [23]

2013

'We don't want two-thirds. We want three-thirds.' [24]

---

21. Answering questions in the National Assembly. Unrevised Hansard, 13 September 2012. Another definitive quote about Zuma's majoritarian attitude to the Constitution, which protects minority rights just as it does majority rights.

22. Speech to the National House of Traditional Leaders in Parliament, 1 November 2012.

23. Ibid.

24. Addressing ANC supporters at a rally at King Zwelithini Stadium in Umlazi. 'ANC wants "three-thirds" in 2014 – Jacob Zuma', *City Press*, 26 July 2013. Zuma's sentiment would be repeated by ANC Secretary General Gwede Mantashe, who would say soon after that the party wanted to 'win everywhere'.

The courts on Jacob Zuma

Jacob Zuma has, during his time in high political and government office, found himself the subject of investigation and legal proceedings. These range from clashes with the law (of which the most infamous is his ever-delayed defence of corruption charges brought against him by the state as a result of his relationship with Schabir Shaik) to other investigations into his conduct, most notably by the public protector.

Zuma has not always been found guilty, whether directly or by implication. Sometimes a not-guilty verdict, as with his 2006 rape trial, is the result. Nevertheless, it is worth listing the findings against Zuma, as they go a considerable way towards defining how history remembers him and stand in stark contrast to the ideals he often espouses as the country's head of state.

2005

'If Zuma could not repay money, how else could he do so than by providing the help of his name and political office as and when it was asked, particularly in the field of government contracted work, which is what Shaik was hoping to benefit from.' [25]

25. Judgment in the High Court of South Africa (Durban and Coastal Local Division), Reportable. Case number: CC27/04. In the matter between the State and Schabir Shaik and others, 31 May 2005.

'These four episodes show in our view that Zuma did in fact intervene to try and assist Shaik's business interests.'[26]

'Accepting then the evidence of these witnesses as the truth of the matters they described, makes the case on Count 1 not just convincing in total, it is really overwhelming.'[27]

2006

'The accused should not have had sexual intercourse with a person so many years younger than himself and furthermore being the child of an old comrade and a woman plus minus his age. The complainant said that in spite of her own attitude that she would not have unprotected sex, it still remains the choice of a person to have unprotected sex. In my judgment that is exactly what she and the accused did that night of 2 November 2005. Having heard the evidence of Prof Martins it is inexcusable that the accused did so. It is totally unacceptable that a man should have unprotected sex with any person other than his regular partner and definitely not with a person who to his knowledge is HIV positive. I do not even want to comment on the effect of a shower after having had unprotected sex. Had Rudyard Kipling known of this case at the time he wrote his poem "If" he might have added the

---

26. High Court Judgment, 31 May 2005.

27. Ibid. Count 1 was the charge that, over a period of time, a total sum of R1 340 078 was paid to Jacob Zuma by Schabir Shaik, that this was done corruptly, the object being to influence Zuma to use his name and political influence for the benefit of Shaik's business enterprises or as an ongoing reward for having done so from time to time.

following: "And if you can control your body and your sexual urges, then you are a man my son."' [28]

'The payments to Zuma, a powerful politician, over a period of more than five years were made calculatingly. Shaik subverted his friendship with Zuma into a relationship of patronage designed to achieve power and wealth. He was brazen and often behaved aggressively and threateningly, using Zuma's name to intimidate people, and particularly potential business partners, into submitting to his will. He sought out people eager to exploit Zuma's power and influence and colluded with them to achieve mutually beneficial results. In our view, the sustained corrupt relationship over the years had the effect that Shaik could use one of the most powerful politicians in the country when it suited him.' [29]

2010

'[T]here is a systemic pattern of noncompliance with the timelines and some of the requirements stipulated in the code by a substantial number of members of the executive, which should be attended to by the Cabinet urgently.' [30]

---

28. Judgment in the High Court of South Africa (Witwatersrand Local Division), Reportable. In the matter between the State and Jacob Gedleyihlekisa Zuma, 8 May 2006. On Zuma's sexual conduct. Zuma would later say, 'The judge was right. The thing is that you have to tell the truth in court, no matter how difficult it is. And you have to take your punishment as well.' See 'Wily old solider keeps his council', *Sunday Argus*, 14 May 2006.

29. Judgment in the Supreme Court of Appeal, Reportable. Case number: 62/06. In the matter between Schabir Shaik and others and the State, 6 November 2006.

30. 'Report of an investigation into an alleged breach of section 5 of the executive ethics code by President JG Zuma', Office of the Public Protector, 21 April 2010. A reference to Zuma's failure properly to disclose his financial interest to Parliament.

'It is of concern that during the inspection of the Register
and interviews with officials charged with its management, it
emerged that the failure to comply with the stipulated time
frames for disclosure is a systemic problem rather than an
isolated incident.' [31]

2011

'I accept that the President is a very busy man, however, when
he is dealing with an office as important as the NDPP, then
time should be taken to get it right.' [32]

'The Minister and the President both made material errors of
fact and law in the process leading up to the appointment of
Mr Simelane.' [33]

'It is clear that the President did not undertake a proper
enquiry … On the available evidence, the President could
not have reached a conclusion favourable to Mr Simelane,
as there were too many questions concerning his integrity
and experience.' [34]

---

31. Office of the Public Protector report, 21 April 2010.

32. Judgment in the Supreme Court of Appeal, Reportable. Case number: (263/11)
[2011] ZASCA 241. In the matter between the Democratic Alliance and the
President of the RSA and others, 1 December 2011. After the High Court found
in favour of Simelane, the Supreme Court overturned the decision in finding that
Zuma had not properly applied his mind to the appointment and that Simelane
was not a fit and proper person for the position of director of public prosecutions.

33. Ibid.

34. Ibid.

CROOKED THINKING ON A CROOKED PATH

JACOB ZUMA, CRIME AND CORRUPTION (AND NKANDLA)

'uSchabir umfowetu.'

For much of his public career, Zuma has been embroiled in one scandal after another. The mother and father of all of these controversies, however, is the Arms Deal and Zuma's relationship with Schabir Shaik, a man convicted of various counts of corruption. Those charges revolved to a large degree around Shaik's relationship with Zuma and monies paid to him; but, while Shaik has paid a high price, Zuma has never faced his day in court, having used every legal means at his disposal to avoid answering the charges brought against him (some 700, including corruption, bribery and racketeering).

But there have been other controversies too. His inappropriate relationship with the Gupta family, a powerful business influence in the country, and the upgrading of his private residence in Nkandla, KwaZulu-Natal, have done little to temper the view that Zuma is morally compromised in some fundamental manner.

Despite this, Zuma has wasted no time, on numerous occasions, speaking about crime and corruption as if entirely unaffected by questions relating to his personal record. One day, he waxes lyrical about the need to renew the country's commitment to fighting a culture of crime and corruption; the next, he defends R250 million worth of public money being spent on, among other things, a swimming pool at his private compound – both with an entirely straight face. This defence did not hold up to independent investigation, however, and was damned from one end to the other by the public protector.

This sort of doublespeak has led to a range of contradictory quotes: an ostensible defence of transparency and accountability on one hand and tortuous explanations for his personal conduct on the other. Sometimes, each component contradicts itself. Take the Arms Deal, for instance. In 2004, arguing against the establishment of a commission of inquiry, he would say of his detractors that '[t]hey are just imagining a problem'. By 2012, his position had changed dramatically, however. Not only would he establish such a commission, but he would defend its necessity by saying that '[t]he arms deal in this country has been an experience that we must all learn from'. As with HIV/Aids, Zuma generally learns such lessons when they are politically convenient.

But perhaps the contradiction peaked, if only in retrospect, in 2002, when Zuma headed the government's moral regeneration movement. As its face, he publicly put forward a number of well-meaning ethical guidelines, only to render each one of them, without exception, profoundly hypocritical by his later behaviour.

Much like Zuma's attitude to respect – which he believes is due to him by virtue of his position – he seems to believe that, as president, patronage and privilege are his by right. He is correct, to a point. And that's the problem. He seems incapable of knowing where to draw a line in the sand – at what point does patronage become influence, and privilege become inappropriate self-indulgence?

His inability to distinguish such things has had consequences not only for his presidency but for his cabinet at large. The general conduct of the executive has come to mirror the arrogance and disdain that Zuma has shown for the necessary ethical prudence and good governance alike, defined as it is by issues like 'blue-light bullies' and five-star hotel accommodation during a period that demanded fiscal prudence.

In turn, he has maintained an iron grip on the criminal justice cluster in the cabinet. He has manned it with allies he deems most loyal to him and who – for the most part, despite the myriad changes he has made to the cabinet during his tenure – have remained in their positions. One level down, however, loyalty has come at a price. Neither the director of public prosecutions (Menzi Simelane) nor the police commissioner (Bheki Cele) elected by Zuma to fulfil his government's mandate lasted long, with incompetence and misconduct bringing their terms to a premature end.

Corruption has been, and always will be, more difficult to define than crime. Ethical corruption in particular is difficult to prove, for it has the built-in benefit of not, technically, being illegal. Corruption and crime do, however, share a mutual moral foundation – disregard for the values that underpin the principles that define the rule of law and give it life. So, it is fitting to merge Zuma's remarks on these issues, as each issue speaks to his standing in the public mind as a moral authority.

Zuma on criminality and corruption

1999

'No, the President has not taken any steps to investigate the
allegations [into irregularities in the Arms Deal]. Government
is satisfied that the entire weapons procurement process has
been an open and transparent procedure. The negotiating
team ensured that every aspect of the negotiations was carried
out in a responsible and accountable manner. The team
reported to the Minister's committee every step of the way.
The committee is chaired by the President who is familiar with
the detail of the tender.'[1]

'[T]he Minister of Defence did his best [to address the issue of
corruption in the Arms Deal]. He addressed the House on the
matter and that closed the chapter as far as that matter was
concerned.'[2]

'In relation to the issue [of whether I should take this up with
the President] ... I think if we did that, this Parliament would
end up with a lot of unnecessary work, because any individual
could sit somewhere, anonymously raise any heavy question

---

1. Answering questions in the National Assembly. Hansard, 20 October 1999,
   pp. 1100–1102. This quote, and the three that follow in notes 2, 3 and 4, are all taken
   from the same question-time address and, jointly and severally, constitute one of
   Zuma's many defences of the government's investigation into the Strategic Defence
   Procurement Package and a refusal to establish a commission of inquiry. They are
   worth comparing with his 2012 announcement that the government would, indeed,
   establish such a commission, after more than ten years of public pressure.

2. Ibid.

and then just expect this Parliament to discuss it. How far does one go in investigating all those questions? I think that this Parliament should be saying that such matters should not come to it … I do not think we should follow that route, otherwise this Parliament could end up discussing rumours and allegations that do not exist.'[3]

'[W]e are satisfied that the process was transparent every step of the way. Following up those rumours, which is what the hon member is saying should be done, is unnecessary. We cannot stand and follow up rumours, really. I do not know why we should be persuaded to follow up all rumours that may come our way.'[4]

2000

'Government will only be satisfied once corruption has been eradicated from the public sector at all levels.'[5]

'This government has taken a number of steps to deal with corruption. These include … [t]he establishment of the Special Investigating Unit, the Public Protector and the Office for Serious Economic Offences …'[6]

---

3. Hansard, 20 October 1999, pp. 1100–1102.

4. Ibid.

5. Answering questions in the National Assembly. Hansard, 17 May 2000, p. 1677. Zuma went on to state: 'We know that in the apartheid period, corruption was endemic, but the people of the country knew very little about it because of the suppression of information and the almost total lack of transparency. However, that does not in any way mitigate corruption in our democratic society; it only makes the task much harder.'

6. Ibid. Zuma praised the Scorpions in 2000. Later, the government shut the unit down.

'I think it is important to say that public servants, in particular, more than anybody else, ought to be aware that they should be more upright and transparent in so far as the use of public funds is concerned.' [7]

'I would like to assure the hon member and this house that there is no tension between the National Police Commissioner of the SA Police Service and the National Director of Public Prosecutions. Both have assured me that there is a very good working relationship between their two offices.' [8]

'… I can certainly give the assurance to this House that there is no abuse of any regulation, rule or law in the context of the operation of the Scorpions. We do have existing policing rules that they are utilising at the moment, as well as those that determine how the justice department operates. At the moment they are operating within the laws. We should have absolutely no fear that they could be out of bounds and abuse the rules because they are operating within the rules of the country.' [9]

---

7. Hansard, 17 May 2000, p. 1677. A good example of the detachment Zuma seems able to generate between his own, compromised standing and the requirement that, like Caesar's wife, public officials be beyond reproach.

8. Ibid. This quote and the following two (notes 9 and 10) are all a response to the following question: '[A]rising out of the hon Deputy President's reply, I would like to know in terms of what set of rules the Scorpions are operating at the moment if there is no legislative framework. Can the Deputy President give an absolute assurance to this house that there is no abuse of power and no undermining of constitutional principles? The National Director said the Scorpions are the police, but they get their money from the Department of Justice.'

9. Ibid.

'[T]he department which is responsible for the Scorpions is the Department of Justice. That is where the Scorpions are controlled from at this point.' [10]

2002

'… I do not belong to those politicians who make mistakes and believe that that is how politicians operate. I think that politicians ought to be exemplary in what they do. That is what the politicians should strive for, if they are not doing that. I am not among those who condemn politicians. I think that politicians deal with matters and I am sure that even political parties might probably differ, who knows, in terms of how they handle things.' [11]

'I am not certain about the ranking of South Africa in as far as crime is concerned. What people miss is the transparency of South Africa. Other countries are not as transparent at all, and they have very high crime rates. I wish that we would not just believe what is said about our country. There are countries where children go to school by helicopters, because if they were to use cars, they would certainly be kidnapped. We have not reached that level yet. I want us as South Africans, when it comes to whatever ranking other institutions give us, not to take it as the truth.' [12]

---

10. Hansard, 17 May 2000, p. 1677. The independence of the Scorpions became an issue of legal concern in a trial involving former Director of Public Prosecutions Vusi Pikoli, with the court later confirming that it should not, as Zuma intimates, report to the executive as this violated the constitutional requirement for a separation of powers between the executive and the prosecuting authority.

11. Answering questions in the National Assembly. Hansard, 13 March 2002, p. 335. In response to a question about the moral regeneration summit.

12. Answering questions in the National Assembly. Hansard, 13 November 2002, pp. 5027–5028. A quote that is typical of the kind of denial that, as in the case of Zimbabwe and quiet diplomacy, Zuma inherited from Mbeki. The thinking seems to be that either South Africa has the worst crime rate in the world, or everything is okay; similarly, unless children are being transported in helicopters, we should not express too much concern.

'The allegations [that I tried to secure a R500 000 protection bribe from a French arms company] are unfounded and completely baseless.' [13]

2003

'… I think I've denied it in the newspapers which have published this allegation. I don't know whether the hon member reads some newspapers and not others because I did deny that.' [14]

'We have set a firm foundation to fight corruption … the most important thing is that we have a system to deal with it and, who comes to the net is not the issue, it could be anyone.' [15]

'We're probably the first government in the world to have taken corruption so seriously.' [16]

'With regards to myself, well, I don't deal with rumours. I don't know what you want me to say on the rumours you say there about my name. How do you answer rumours? If people start rumours, how do you know what is indeed a rumour or not a rumour? I think there is a process that in any sensible country and state is followed. Investigations are done, charges are preferred and people are taken to court, and then people answer. I don't think you want this country to be engaged in

---

13. A statement from Zuma in a 'rushed' interview. 'Corruption allegations are without foundation, Zuma insists', *The Star*, 10 December 2002.

14. Answering questions in the National Assembly. Hansard, 12 March 2003, p. 291. In response to the question, 'You are alleged to have solicited a payment of R500 000 per annum from an arms dealer. Instead of staying quiet, now is the moment to protest your innocence before parliament and before the people of South Africa.'

15. 'Zuma: HRC report does not give credit where it is due', *Sunday Independent*, 27 April 2003.

16. Ibid.

the process of debating any rumour that arises. Anybody can start a rumour about you. Is that reality? I think you should allow a process that is legal and transparent to take its course, and then make your necessary comments.' [17]

'[M]y understanding is that a person has the right to be presumed innocent until proven guilty. In this instance no one has been found guilty of anything. Allegations have been made and investigated. According to the National Director of Public Prosecutions and the senior counsel he consulted, I will not be prosecuted because they do not think there is a winnable case. As far as I am concerned, I know I have not engaged in any immoral activities and therefore do not see the need to relinquish my responsibilities in the moral regeneration movement.' [18]

'The Deputy President has not been weakened by anything because he has committed no crime, and is therefore not going

---

17. Answering questions in the National Assembly. Hansard, 21 May 2003, pp. 1927–1928. In response to a DA question about 'unresolved questions' about the deputy president's involvement with Thales, the French arms manufacturer from which he was accused of taking a bribe, as evidenced by an encrypted facsimile.

18. Answering questions in the National Assembly. Hansard, 10 September 2003, p. 3496. The verdict in the Shaik trial (in June 2005) changed that, and President Thabo Mbeki acted to remove the deputy president from his position. The Shaik trial also confirmed that Zuma did receive a series of bribes from Shaik, which influenced him to act – the Constitutional Court found, in a unanimous verdict in a subsequent hearing in May 2008, that the state had established 'as a matter of fact' that Zuma's former financial adviser had received multi-million-rand benefits 'as a result of Mr Zuma's support for Mr Shaik and his companies'. In doing so, the Constitutional Court accepted the Supreme Court of Appeal's finding that Shaik's payments to Zuma were made 'in order to influence Mr Zuma to promote Mr Shaik's business interests'.

to relinquish, as I said in my first answer, any position
or responsibility. There is absolutely no need for that.' [19]

2004

'[The Arms Deal] is another imagined issue. It's just a figment
of the imagination, because hon members have not paid
attention to what benefits have been brought by the arms deal
in terms of the industry of the country. Again, they would
be imagining it. I know that they have been chasing to find
something. Up to this day, nobody has found anything. They've
been chasing it in the sea, in the sky and everywhere. Nothing
has been found. What is the problem?' [20]

2005

'With regard to the allegations, the hon member knows that
these allegations have been made. I do not have the facts
about the allegations. This government has been the first
government in this country to wage a war against corruption.
Never in the past was there any government that did that.
Whenever there has been a discovery of corruption, it has
acted. Where there has been an investigation, at whatever

---

19. Answering questions in the National Assembly. Hansard, 10 September 2003,
    p. 3499.

20. Answering questions in the National Assembly. Hansard, 25 February 2004,
    pp. 118–119. Perhaps the ultimate government defence of its refusal to set up a
    commission of inquiry into the Arms Deal.

level, it has never interfered. It has allowed the due process of law to continue.' [21]

'[W]e would have a funny government if it chased rumours every day on what appeared in the newspapers.' [22]

'*uSchabir umfowetu* [Schabir is my brother]. Saying I must cut ties with him is like saying I must disown my own brother.' [23]

2006

'It's unfortunate that, despite readiness to defend myself and clear my name, the NPA failed to present its case when called upon to do so.' [24]

---

21. Answering questions in the National Assembly. Hansard, 8 June 2005, pp. 1403–1404. This remark and the one that follows (note 22) were made in response to questions about Oilgate and the allegation that the ANC had effectively funnelled R11 million worth of taxpayers' money through PetroSA, via a subsidiary (Imvume Management) into the ruling party's 2004 election coffers. It is a remarkable statement, not only because the ANC government went out of its way on crush any investigation into the matter – from the public protector, through to SCOPA, to the police and to Parliament – but because, some three years later, outgoing ANC Treasurer General Mendi Msimang told the ANC national conference in Polokwane that the ANC had returned the money: 'Indeed we did receive a donation of R11 million in the normal course of our fundraising and, when it appeared, there was a dispute around it ... We immediately returned the entire donation to the donor in two instalments ...'. See 'ANC reveals it did pay back Oilgate cash', *Cape Argus*, 18 December 2007.

22. Ibid.

23. 'Remembering a man laid bare by loyalty', *Sowetan*, 15 June 2005. Shaik was found guilty on two counts of corruption and one count of fraud. He was sentenced to 15 years' imprisonment on each of the two counts of corruption, as well as three years on the count of fraud, but released on parole, for medical reasons, supposedly because his death was imminent in March 2009, after serving just two years.

24. 'Zuma – improper motives drove my prosecution', South African Press Association, 22 September 2006.

'Our media, which is very open and report on really everything, tend to exaggerate the crime issue ... This is why one gets the impression that we have much more crime than other countries. In our case the media goes too far when it comes to openness.'[25]

2007

'I never said that. That was someone else. I said, "In my case, let justice take its course." And that's all. I never said anything about wanting any days in court. That's rubbish.'[26]

2008

'KEANE: A lot of people think you're a crook ...

ZUMA: Is that so? *(laughs)*. I want to see those people so they can tell me why they think I'm a crook.

KEANE: Well, there's a whole army of prosecutors who clearly think it.

ZUMA: Eh-ha? Is that so? Serious?

KEANE: Are you a crook?

ZUMA: Me? Well, I don't know, I must go to a dictionary and learn what a crook is. I've never been a crook.

KEANE: Somebody who takes money from other people for corrupt purposes?

ZUMA: Have I ever done so?

KEANE: I'm asking you.

---

25. In an interview with the German magazine *Der Spiegel*. '"The West is bent out of shape"', *Der Spiegel*, 20 December 2006.

26. In an interview with his biographer, Jeremy Gordin. 'Umqombothi at Jacob's place', *Sunday Tribune*, 25 November 2007. Zuma was asked about reports that he had allegedly said he wanted his day in court. He faced 783 counts of corruption but the charges were dropped by the National Prosecuting Authority.

ZUMA: No, I think that's a mistake you guys have made and I've said, I can't have two trials – trial by the media and trial by court. I'm saying I'm not a crook. I have never been a crook. I will never be a crook.' [27]

2009

'Criminals don't take an oath to do warning shots. If you take a gun out to me, that intent is more than clear, the next thing the criminal is going to shoot at me. That intent is very clear … We have an abnormal criminal problem in South Africa. We must therefore apply extraordinary measures.' [28]

'No police officer has the permission to shoot suspects in the circumstances other than those provided by the law. The law does not give the police a licence to kill.' [29]

2012

'The arms deal in this country has been an experience that we must all learn from. In future, if we were to undertake such a task, we would certainly look at what happened in our experience and take the correct steps in order to eliminate some of the things that might have caused problems. There's no doubt about it.' [30]

---

27. In an interview by Fergal Keane for the BBC programme *Panorama*, 13 February 2008.

28. 'Criminals don't do warning shots', *Sowetan*, 30 September 2009. Another Zuma contradiction. His 'extraordinary measures' comment appears to be an endorsement of the shoot-to-kill policy advocated by numerous people in the executive. But, after a public outcry, Zuma would backpedal only a few months later. See the next quote.

29. 'Zuma does damage control on latest shoot-to-kill controversy', *Saturday Star*, 14 November 2009.

30. Answering questions in the National Assembly. Unrevised Hansard, 19 March 2012. On 15 September 2011, after more than a decade of obfuscation and

2013

'We're not forcing people … you can support and be a
supporter, but if you go beyond that and become a member,
[and] if you're a businessman, your business will multiply …
Everything you touch will multiply. I've always said that a wise
businessperson will support the ANC … because supporting
the ANC means you're investing very well in your business.'[31]

'Honourable member, it is because any member of the public
in South Africa and our borders is free to contact members of
my cabinet, the executive or the public direct. It is in line with
the ethos of our administration, which promotes an open and
accessible government.'[32]

'The honourable member who asked the question made a very
clear statement that every human being has a right to have
friends with whoever. We are not in [a] state that bans people
because they've got friends [*sic*] with others.'[33]

---

denial, President Zuma announced that he would appoint a commission of
inquiry to investigate allegations of wrongdoing in the Strategic Defence
Procurement Package, more infamously known as the Arms Deal. In making
the announcement, the president was curt and offered little in the way of a
substantive explanation for his decision, saying only that 'closure on this subject
will be in the public interest'. This would be his explanation for the decision. It
stands in stark contrast to his remarks on the same subject in 2000 and 2004.

31. Said during an address at the ANC's 101st Anniversary Gala Dinner, Durban,
12 January 2013.

32. Answering questions in the National Assembly. Unrevised Hansard, Transcript
of the reply by President Jacob Zuma to question for oral reply in the National
Assembly, 19 June 2013. Zuma was being questioned about whether he knew
about the decision to allow a Gupta-hired plane containing 200 guests to
land at Waterkloof Air Force Base for a private wedding ceremony at Sun
City. Waterkloof is a National Key Point. Zuma's defence, as ever, was to
feign ignorance and talk in generics rather than in terms of moral or ethical
responsibility.

33. Ibid.

'No, no, no, there are many of my friends who have committed many things.' [34]

'For example, on that landing, you will remember, people were saying, "the president must explain", I had nothing to do with it. You can see how much it is taken out of context. That people use certain things to achieve certain things.' [35]

'You can see the exaggeration that comes with all of this. I am sure there are many people who commit a lot of other things, planes land in Lanseria, wrongly – no story about it. Precisely because this family knows Zuma, then it becomes a big story. I think at times it is an exaggeration of things.' [36]

34. Unrevised Hansard, 19 June 2013. Asked if he was embarrassed about his friends in the Gupta family and the landing of their private plane at a military air base and national key point.

35. Ibid. Also, on the Guptas (see note 32).

36. Ibid. (see note 32).

Nkandla: A home away from home

As president, Jacob Zuma has five official residences available to him: Mahlamba Ndlopfu (Pretoria); Genadendal (Cape Town); Oliver Tambo House (Pretoria); Highstead (Cape Town) and Dr John L Dube House (formerly King's House, Durban). In 2009/2010 it was revealed that the upkeep of these five homes costs about R26 million per year.

However, it is one of his two private homes (he has one in Forest Town, Johannesburg) that grabbed public attention. It was revealed that the state had spent some R250 million on Zuma's rural homestead in Nkandla, KwaZulu-Natal, ostensibly to upgrade its security. However, not all of that money was directly related to security, despite the state's best protestations. Money was spent on everything from cattle kraals to a 'fire pool' (a swimming pool doubling as a fire-safe haven). Nkandla is a scandal that will define Zuma's legacy.

Zuma's defence, and that of the government, has always rested on two claims. First, that Zuma was unaware of the systems and decisions that resulted in the huge security spend and that, essentially, he is not responsible for them. Second, that Zuma and his family had footed the bill for every part of the homestead's upgrade that was not security-related. Zuma has generally kept a low profile on this subject but, when he was forced to address it, he stuck rigidly to these two lines, as did the government: a technical defence that, whatever its veracity, negates any ethical introspection.

That is the official line. Smuggled through in this line is the subtle suggestion of racism (that black people may not build and are not entitled to a home) and special pleading (that he is a victim, unfairly targeted by a malicious media and opposition). Zuma has combined the official and the unofficial seamlessly in putting forward his defence. In a country where victimhood is rife, Zuma plays the role of the ultimate victim with aplomb, and it is a role that has brought him high office and acted as a political bulwark against any acceptance of personal responsibility.

Ultimately, however, all of this was rendered redundant by Public Protector Thuli Madonsela, whose final report into the Nkandla scandal reads like a 400-page constitutional horror story. Madonsela made a raft of adverse findings against everyone from Zuma, through members of his executive, to the lowlier government officials who handled the project on the ground. At the centre of it all, however, was Zuma – the infected heart that pumped personal indulgence to all of these minor organs.

Zuma has always enjoyed the benefit of party faithful who have dissociated his personal conduct from the ANC brand. Nkandla joins a growing list of substantial controversies to have immersed Zuma, but few have affected the ANC's overall support; those that do cause only minimal damage. History will be the final arbiter in this regard: a bitter pill to swallow for many vested in the contemporary implications. When history does look back on Zuma's term in office, Nkandla will be the metaphor that best captures Zuma's personal politics and the relationship between these and a more general and pervasive corruption and maladministration problem that plagues the country.

2006

'It's really wonderful there. I walk around, talk to people, think – though there were always people arriving from Johannesburg to bother me.' [37]

'We didn't send invitations. In our culture, we don't send out cards. People just arrive and enjoy the event with us.' [38]

'The Jacob Zuma you know today was formed by what I learnt here as a child. It was here in Nkandla I learnt about respect.' [39]

---

37. 'Wily old soldier keeps his council', *Sunday Argus*, 14 May 2006.

38. 'Zuma happy to be a T-shirt pop idol', *Sowetan*, 12 July 2006. After his not-guilty verdict in his rape trial, Zuma threw what he described as the 'mother of all feasts', at Nkandla.

39. To supporters who gathered at his Nkandla residence for a party to celebrate his rape trial's not-guilty verdict. 'Zuma bedank sy ondersteuners op groot partytjie', *Beeld*, 17 July 2006.

2007

'I blossom when I'm there … Some of the old people come
to me when I am there and say, "you don't need these people
(security) when you are here … at Nkandla". I feel home – I
smell no danger.' [40]

'This is where I regenerate and reconnect. This is where I
come back to myself. This is a particularly Zulu environment
and yet this is where I become a South African. If I become too
high-flying, this is the place that puts me back on my feet.' [41]

2008

'Today is not just Christmas for the kids but for the adults too.' [42]

2009

'Your deed to overwhelmingly elect me the president of
the country hugely humbled me. But I want to make an
undertaking today that I will not forget you.' [43]

'Some of the lessons I learnt from the village and its people
could not be obtained from any university. They taught me

40. 'Zuma opens up to us', *The Citizen*, 20 March 2007. Things would change and that
    sense of freedom would soon be lost – so much so that, on becoming president,
    Zuma would need security upgrades worth R250 million.

41. In an interview with his biographer, Jeremy Gordin. 'Umqombothi at Jacob's
    place', *Sunday Tribune*, 25 November 2007. Zuma also said of Nkandla, 'But look
    around you. What a wonderful and beautiful place this is. And the people are so
    friendly. Can you blame me for liking to come here?'

42. 'Zuma plays Santa Claus for orphans', South African Press Association,
    30 December 2008. At his annual Christmas party in Nkandla, Zuma would reveal
    a new R13.5 million multipurpose centre for the community. 'We did this to bring
    service to the people,' he said.

43. After he won the presidency in 2009, Zuma held a party for 30 000 people in
    Nkandla, including many high-ranking public office-bearers. This was said to the
    crowd. 'Party time at Zuma village', *The Star*, 8 June 2009. It was reported that
    every helicopter in the province was hired out for the event.

to respect, to listen and to be humble myself.'[44]

2012

'Hon Speaker, hon member, let me make one thing quite clear from the outset. I have noted all sorts of public comments to the effect that the government built my home in Nkandla. My residence in Nkandla has been paid for by the Zuma family. All the buildings and every room we use in that residence were built by ourselves as a family and not by government. I have never asked government to build a home for me, and it has not done so. The government has not built a home for me.'[45]

'A wrong impression is being given that the government has built a home for me. It is not true; people are speaking without knowing and therefore saying I've spent so much money of the government ... It is unfair and I don't want to use harsher words, because you believe that people like me can't build a home.'[46]

'Today, hon Speaker, I have the opportunity to explain this, because my name is being used wrongly. My family is being undermined, by the very hon members who do not ask what actually happened. I feel very aggrieved, and I must tell you for the first time.'[47]

---

44. 'Party time at Zuma village', *The Star*, 8 June 2009.

45. Answering questions in the National Assembly. Unrevised Hansard, Transcript of the reply by President Jacob Zuma to question for oral reply in the National Assembly, 15 November 2012. In response to a question from DA Parliamentary leader Lindiwe Mazibuko, who asked '[w]hether he instructed his Minister of Public Works to cease all building on his Nkandla home pending the outcome of an investigation announced by the Public Protector; if not, why not; if so, when?'

46. Ibid.

47. Ibid.

'You then have leaders of political parties who do not know whether they are provincial or national, taking trips to come and photograph my home and make a laughing stock of my family. I take exception to this! You must deal with the facts you know.' [48]

2014

'People have short memories. A few years ago, when I built my homestead, they said I'd used French money. They have forgotten about it. The very place they [are] now showing where they say I have supposedly used government money. It's the same place. This is unfair.' [49]

'They want to show I am corrupt – that Zuma has eaten R250 million, whoever is making that allegation. They have never worried themselves to check … they leak unverified reports, knowing very well this is the very homestead that was once the subject of discussion. Now they are repeating it. It is unfair.' [50]

'The government came very late to introduce security features at the level that they were being introduced before Zuma became the president. It was their confidential things. They never discussed with anyone of the family. So even if you wanted to talk, the family didn't know. The very government

48. Unrevised Hansard, 15 November 2012. A reference to a visit by DA leader Helen Zille to the homestead.

49. Interview with the *Sunday Independent*. 'Nkandla critics are unfair – Zuma', *Sunday Independent*, 9 February 2014.

50. Ibid.

… they are the ones who know better.'[51]

'I don't deal with it. But where it was necessary for them to come and ask questions, I was always there.'[52]

'Not at all.'[53]

'The Presidency has noted the release of the final report of the Public Protector today, 19 March 2014, into the security upgrades at the Nkandla private residence of President Jacob Zuma. One of the key successes of our democracy is the Constitution with its important features such as the institutions supporting and strengthening constitutional democracy. These include the Chapter 9 Institutions. President Zuma reaffirms the important role of the Chapter 9 institutions and emphasises that the country should take pride in their existence, as we celebrate 20 years of freedom and democracy and guard against the abuse and misuse of these institutions. The President has consistently been concerned about the allegations of impropriety around procurement in the Nkandla project. It is for this reason that government appointed an Inter-Ministerial Task Team. The report has been made public and it has also been presented to parliament. In addition, last December, President Zuma

---

51. 'Nkandla critics are unfair – Zuma', *Sunday Independent*, 9 February 2014.

52. Ibid.

53. 'Zuma talks Nkandla, Malema and Guptagate', eNCA, 16 February 2014. Zuma was asked whether he should resign over the Nkandla scandal. He went on to say, somewhat cryptically, 'I should have thought of giving up the struggle when it was very tough. Never.'

directed the Special Investigating Unit to probe alleged maladministration committed during the implementation of the security upgrades at Nkandla. In this context, the Public Protector's report will be an additional tool which will fall under the consideration of President Zuma in addressing allegations of maladministration.' [54]

'All I did was to build my father's house and they are chasing after me for that. I'm from Nkandla, I will never leave that place. When I retire I will return there. I never asked anyone [to help me with the upgrades]. I have wives and so I needed to extend my homestead to accommodate my large family. That is not a crime. They say I'm corrupt and I built my house with taxpayers' money ... I never did that.' [55]

'I've done nothing wrong. Even if they look underneath a tree or a rock they won't find anything against me. I'm not

---

54. 'Media Statement: Presidency notes the release of the Public Protector Report', 19 March 2014. This was the first official response from the Presidency to the report of Public Protector Thuli Madonsela into the Nkandla scandal. Madonsela found that the upgrades to the president's property would take an estimated R246 million to complete and that many of them, supposedly undertaken in the name of security, were, in fact, personal indulgences built in violation of a raft of procedural requirements. The president, she found, was obliged to pay back a 'reasonable percentage' of some of the costs. Among them: the swimming pool, cattle kraal, amphitheatre, visitors' centre and chicken run. She found it could be construed that Zuma had misled, but not willingly, that he had 'tacitly accepted' the changes, failed to ask the appropriate questions and that, as a result of all of this, he had 'improperly benefited' from the upgrades and contradicted the values of the Executive Members Ethics Act. Many others involved in the project were found to have breached no end of technical, legal and ethical constraints. She called it the 'toxic concoction of a lack of leadership, a lack of control and focused self-interest'.

guilty. Investigations have been done and they found nothing against me.' [56]

'They searched and investigated and finished but they did not find anything. What I am saying is that this case does not even exist.' [57]

'They did this without telling me. So why should I pay for something I did not ask for.' [58]

55. Speaking to a small crowd of elderly people in Gugulethu, Cape Town. After 11 days, Zuma broke his silence on the public protector's findings. 'JZ: I've done nothing wrong', *The Times*, 31 March 2014.
56. Ibid. A reference to criminal charges laid against Zuma by the Democratic Alliance, in response to Madonsela's report.
57. '"I did nothing wrong"', *The New Age*, 31 March 2014. Additional reportage on the same Cape Town address cited in notes 55 and 56.
58. 'I didn't ask for Nkandla upgrade – Zuma', South African Press Association, 31 March 2014. Additional reportage.

SPIN DOCTORING
THE ZUMA SICKNESS

JACOB ZUMA AND CRISIS MANAGEMENT

'The words have regrettably been taken out of context and blown completely out of proportion.'

Never before in South Africa's recent history has a senior member of the executive been as reliant on his spokespeople as Jacob Zuma. He has already been through his fair share, in government and the ANC. Jimmy Manyi, Zizi Kodwa, Vincent Magwenya, Carl Niehaus – many had come and gone before the two incumbents, Mac Maharaj and Jackson Mthembu, settled in their positions.

The routine is now fairly standard: Zuma says something controversial, nonsensical or contradictory and either Mac Maharaj (if said in Zuma's capacity as president) or Jackson Mthembu (if said as ANC leader) is deployed to clean up the mess. There have been others, but, for the most part, these two are the verbal doctors on 24-hour call, should Zuma suffer some kind of rhetorical breakdown – which happens rather often.

Maharaj and Mthembu employ various tricks to explain away the president's bumblings. One of the most common is to suggest there was some confusion – a mis-understanding born of the fact that Zuma is not a first-language English speaker and, often, says some of his most controversial things in isiZulu. That might go some way towards placating the inevitable outrage that follows but, viewed over time, almost every dubious position the president takes is repeated by him elsewhere in another shape or form. There are very few Zuma remarks that can be dismissed as a complete aberration. Most are consistent with a theme.

Another response is to appeal to authority, and culture is the source to which his spokespeople turn. Zuma is a traditionalist, they argue, and one must respect tradition, as if every cultural practice – from virginity testing to an appreciation for the arts – enjoys a moral equivalence. This also suggests that there is no objective, universal moral code to which South Africa subscribes. There is: the Bill of Rights. And the Constitution should be the lens through which we evaluate any cultural practice. The ANC has gone some way towards subverting this requirement, however, and, for many, political correct-ness now demands that the Constitution be interpreted from the point of view of tradition. Certainly that view is often implied in the defences offered up by Zuma's political handlers.

There are other tricks – for example, the suggestion that a remark was merely a metaphor and not meant to be taken literally. This has been used before to defend Zuma's many and varied religious utterances. But, here, Zuma tries to have his cake and eat it. For the most part, he is speaking to the rural poor when he alludes to religion, a constituency often deeply immersed in superstitious and mystical beliefs. Members of this constituency do not just take Zuma seriously – they believe much more besides. And Zuma knows this.

Zuma almost always addresses two different worlds – the world of mysticism and magic on one hand, and a modern democracy on the other. When they meet, he explains away the one with references to the other; but those who occupy each respective world hear one of only two things: a man who believes that God and the ancestors talk to him about their political preferences, or a man who is out of touch with the key democratic tenets he is supposed to embody. Both often lead to much confusion in the mainstream media.

When rhetorical sleight of hand isn't used, there is straightforward denial ('The president never said that'), or the suggestion that the media is deliberately distorting Zuma's words ('This has been blown out of all proportion'). One can search long and hard; only on the rarest of occasions will one find the phrase 'The president was wrong and apologises', and this usually only after a national scandal.

Zuma's spokespeople often become the story. The unofficial version, with its big headline and appropriate reaction, precedes the 'official' version, hard-cased in democratic rhetoric and always feigning reason and common sense. The contrast, however, couldn't be starker.

It must be difficult for Zuma. He has built much of his political career on his authenticity. His great appeal to many is that he is ordinary, the everyday man. To have his beliefs constantly reworded and remoulded into something more palatable must irk him greatly. No doubt, that is why, over time, he simply says the same thing again and again. Political marketing can do great things for one's reputation but, given enough time in the public spotlight, it is almost impossible to suppress permanently one's authentic nature.

Zuma and his spin doctors

2004

'The expression the Deputy President used was a manner of speech which is used in a number of ways in a number of different languages.'[1]

2009

'The ANC has not equated itself to God and has never pretended to be God. We are taken aback by the Bishop's sacrilege.'[2]

'[The president's remarks] should be understood in the context of the president's confidence in South Africans who have – in the past four successive elections – voted overwhelmingly for the ANC.'[3]

2010

'There is no contradiction. Maybe it's a matter of semantics that's getting people excited.'[4]

---

1. ANC spokesperson Smuts Ngonyama. 'ANC shrugs off criticism of "Jesus" remark made by Zuma', South African Press Association, 16 March 2004. Zuma had said that 'the ANC will rule South Africa until Jesus comes back'.

2. General ANC statement, in response to Desmond Tutu, 2 April 2009. Replying to Zuma's various utterances about the ANC, God and Jesus, Archbishop Desmond Tutu had said that 'you [the ANC government] are not God'.

3. ANC spokesperson Brian Sokutu. 'Church is "privatizing" Jesus', *The Times*, 24 June 2009. Another defence of Zuma's comments about the ANC and Jesus.

4. Spokesperson for the Presidency, Vincent Magwenya. 'Spokesman stands by president', *The Citizen*, 13 January 2010. Magwenya was defending Zuma's suggestion that he had seen no presidential pardon application from Schabir Shaik when, in fact, the Presidency itself had formally acknowledged such an application a year earlier. There was, indeed, much confusion.

'The state only provides reasonable administrative, logistical and other support to the spouses to enable them to meet the expectations related to the nature of the office of the president.'[5]

2011

'If, indeed, the use of the word Heaven in a figurative expression was deemed inappropriate by the South African society and the world at large, expressions such as "MARRIAGE MADE IN HEAVEN", "HEAVENLY VOICES" and "SWEETS FROM HEAVEN" – to name a few – would not exist. The figurative weekend expression by the President remains figurative and metaphoric. We are, therefore, in agreement with the President that not voting for the ANC is tantamount to throwing your vote in burning hell.'[6]

'The stereotyping and pigeonholing does not constitute [the] fairness and objectivity that is expected of the media and misinforms the public. The President takes decisions independently, informed by the facts that are placed before him. The pigeonholing of the President misleads the public and also kills critical thinking in the media and public space.'[7]

---

5. Communications Advisor to the President, Zizi Kodwa. 'Wives no state burden', letter to the editor, *Business Day*, 9 November 2010. Zuma had revealed, in response to a Parliamentary question, that the amount spent on spousal support unit was R15 517 500 per year.

6. ANC spokesperson Jackson Mthembu. 'ANC Statement: President Jacob Zuma's figurative expression amounts to no blasphemy', 6 February 2011. Zuma had said, 'When you are carrying an ANC membership card, you are blessed. When you get up there, there are different cards used but when you have an ANC card, you will be let through to go to heaven.'

7. Spokesperson for the Presidency, Mac Maharaj. 'Media prone to stereotyping Zuma', *The Citizen*, 21 October 2011. A general plea from Maharaj not to label Zuma unfairly ahead of the ANC's Mangaung elective conference.

'Irresponsible journalism will always find a creative way to mislead, and in this case it inexplicably saw an attack on Christianity in the president's perfectly sound assertion.'[8]

'The president speaks in deep Zulu on occasion and his message is often lost in translation.'[9]

2012

'This must therefore not be viewed as an attempt by government to undermine the independence of the judiciary and the rule of law which are entrenched in our Constitution. This is an exercise that falls within the mandate of the Executive of formulating and reviewing policies of government which seek to advance the transformative character of our Constitution.'[10]

'His spokesman, Mac Maharaj, said Zuma had been speaking in the context of "the need to build cohesive communities and families". He believes strengthening the family is important to enable the building of stronger communities to deal with the many social ills facing society today.'[11]

---

8. ANC Chief Whip Mathole Motshekga. 'Zuma slated for Christianity comments', South African Press Association, 21 December 2011. Zuma had said that 'there were no orphans or old age homes' before Christianity arrived.

9. Ibid. This is the defence that Spokesperson for the Presidency, Mac Maharaj, offered for the same incident.

10. Spokesperson for the Presidency, Mac Maharaj. 'Media Statement: President Zuma's comments on judicial review', 13 February 2012. Zuma had said, 'We don't want to review the Constitutional Court, we want to review its powers.'

11. Spokesperson for the Presidency, Mac Maharaj. 'Zuma's single women views spark anger', *The Mercury*, 23 August 2012. Zuma said in a television interview that '[k]ids are important to a woman because they give extra training to a woman, to be a mother'.

'It appears that the comments by President Jacob Zuma in the National Assembly, that majority rules in a democracy, has been misconstrued by the Democratic Alliance party to mean the minority has less rights in the country. Nothing could be further from the truth … The President was stating a fundamental democratic principle that while all in society may have views, the will of the majority carries the day.' [12]

'The Presidency rejects the ongoing campaign of linking every development around Nkandla village to the person of Zuma.' [13]

'It is mischievous and inaccurate to insinuate that the road was constructed because the president lives there.' [14]

'It was only after he became president that security, medical and other considerations had to be made, as explained by the Minister of Public Works, Thulas Nxesi, on behalf of government.' [15]

'Media reports on the President Zuma's speech on the Traditional Courts Bill to the National House of Traditional Leaders in Cape Town on the 1st of November 2012, has been sensationalized by some newspapers to the point of being grossly misleading.' [16]

12. Spokesperson for the Presidency, Mac Maharaj. 'Media Statement on Democracy remarks by the President', 16 September 2012. A response to Zuma's remark in Parliament that '[y]ou have fewer rights because you are a minority'.

13. Spokesperson for the Presidency, Mac Maharaj. 'Road upgrade "not linked to Zuma"', *The New Age*, 12 October 2012. It had been reported in *The Mercury* that the P15 road to Zuma's homestead village in Nkandla was to be upgraded at a cost of R290 million. Zuma had denied any involvement in the upgrades to the area and his house to a business breakfast hosted by *The New Age* a few days earlier.

14. Ibid.

15. Ibid.

16. Spokesperson for the Presidency, Mac Maharaj. 'Media Statement: President Zuma acknowledged shortcomings in Traditional Courts Bill', 2 November 2012. Zuma had said to Parliament, among other things, 'Let us solve African problems the African way, not the white man's way.'

'[T]he essential message from the President was the need
to decolonise the African mind post-liberation to enable the
previously oppressed African majority to appreciate and love
who they are and uphold their own culture.' [17]

2013

'It is also a fact that the ANC is the only party in South
Africa that has economic and business friendly policies. The
implication of this reality is that if business wants to prosper in
South Africa, they have to support the ANC as their prosperity
is dependent on the ANC being at the helm of South Africa's
government.' [18]

'It is a sad fact that Lindiwe Mazibuko is so naive when it comes
to African traditions that she cannot relate to them. It is our tradition as Africans that if someone gives you something, in return
you thank him/her and wish them prosperity and abundance.' [19]

'The words have regrettably been taken out of context and
blown completely out of proportion … The President then
made the example that it was also not fair to expect Gauteng
roads to be compared to roads in other towns such as
"Pietermaritzburg, Rustenburg, Polokwane or any other town
or national road in Malawi as this was Gauteng, the

---

17. Spokesperson for the Presidency, Mac Maharaj. 'Media Statement: President's
remarks on promoting Ubuntu', 27 December 2012. Zuma was reported as saying
that white people cared more for their dogs than for others and that black women
should not use hair straighteners in an attempt to become 'white'.

18. ANC spokesperson Jackson Mthembu. 'ANC Statement: On the call made by the
DA', 14 January 2013. Said in response to Zuma's comments that everything a
businessperson touches 'will multiply' if he or she supports the ANC.

19. Ibid. In response to criticism from DA Parliamentary leader Lindiwe Mazibuko
about the president's remarks.

heartbeat of South Africa's economy and an international city of commerce and business."' [20]

'The African National Congress places it on record that both the organisation and the President hold the people of Malawi and elsewhere on the continent in high regard. The context in which the statement was made must be clarified in order to understand how the President's comment, which has been mischievously been singled out, arose … It was within this context that the President called on residents of this province to not think and act like others in the country and continent who do not have the unique responsibility and critical role Gauteng has as a gateway to Africa and the industrial and economic hub of South Africa … The African National Congress welcomes the role played by traditional and social media in our national discourse. It is important therefore that those privileged to form opinion on these networks do so with the intention of promoting fair and balanced reporting, a call we believe would not have arisen had the President's comments were [sic] placed in context.' [21]

'I have received numerous calls from Malawians being angry and, after long discussions, they come around and say, yes, let's not make a mountain of a molehill … Let me apologise for that and withdraw it.' [22]

---

20. Spokesperson for the Presidency, Mac Maharaj. 'Media Statement: Presidency corrects distortions in the media', 22 October 2013. Zuma had said that '[w]e can't think like Africans in Africa generally', in defending Gauteng's eTolls.

21. ANC spokesperson Jackson Mthembu. 'Media Statement: Remarks by President Jacob Zuma at Gauteng ANC Manifesto Forum', 22 October 2013.

22. Spokesperson for the Presidency, Mac Maharaj, speaking on Power FM radio on 23 October 2013, in response to the president's comments about Malawi and Gauteng's eTolls. His apology represented an about-turn, given that just the previous day he had referred to the outrage as a 'distortion' (see note 20).

Zuma spinning his own words

On the odd occasion, Jacob Zuma has been prepared to defend himself. He does not have a way with words, as Maharaj does; so, the defence he offers is usually to feign ignorance. If he had suggested something, he would say that he was only encouraging debate and not advocating a particular position. If he had taken a more concrete – albeit controversial – position, he would downplay its seriousness by suggesting that he was merely advocating common sense which, if related in a generic enough fashion, is harmless.

2006

'Firstly, I'm not certain how and why the shower thing was singled out. I did not just voluntarily say I believe a shower takes it [HIV/Aids] away. She asked me why did I need to go and have a shower and I said as an additional measure to me to clean myself, because I knew the type of person I was sleeping with … That's an honest answer I gave. I didn't say, as it has been reported, that showering is a cure for Aids.'[23]

'As I testified in court, under oath, I am HIV negative, having undergone an HIV test in March this year. I wish to state categorically and place on record that I erred in having unprotected sex. I should have known better and I should

---

23. Zuma in an exchange with a television reporter, at a press conference following his not-guilty verdict in his rape trial. "'I didn't say showering is a cure for Aids'", *The Star*, 10 May 2006.

have acted with greater caution and responsibility. For this,
I unconditionally apologise to all the people of this country.' [24]

'I'm not an angel, I live in this world. I think the court is a
different place.' [25]

'I have noted that the statements I made at the Shaka Day
commemoration in kwaDukuza, KwaZulu-Natal on 24
September 2006 have been interpreted in various ways, and
may have hurt and angered the gay and lesbian community
in our country. My remarks were made in the context of the
traditional way of raising children … I said the communal
upbringing of children in the past was able to assist parents to
notice children with a different social orientation. I however
did not intend to have this interpreted as a condemnation of
gays and lesbians … I apologise unreservedly for the pain and
anger that my remarks may have caused.' [26]

2008

'I said there should be dialogue on the matter. As the ANC,
we welcome interaction between the different formations
of organized labour in the country.' [27]

---

24. 'Media Statement by ANC Deputy president Jacob Zuma on his acquittal by the
    Johannesburg High Court May 9 2006', 14 May 2009.

25. Ibid.

26. 'Statement by ANC Deputy President Jacob Zuma on remarks about gay and
    lesbian community', 28 September 2006. The official apology issued by Zuma, in
    response to outrage about his comments that, amongst other things, gay marriage
    was a 'disgrace before God'.

27. Clarifying Statement made on 10 March 2010. See 'Man with more lives than a
    cat', *The Star*, 28 March 2008. Said in response to his comments to the trade union
    Solidarity about affirmative action, in which he suggested that the policy was not
    cast in stone.

2009

'There is no first lady. I think it's an old debate between those
who have been colonised and those who were colonising.
It's a wrong debate which people write long columns about.
There's no magic about the "first lady", if you've got wives,
what is important is that you are able to deal with them.
If there is an occasion, one day we will have the wife we
are with, another day we will have another one, it's not an
issue.'[28]

'It's an expression to mean the ANC is strong. I have read the
other parties' manifestos. I do not think they offer anything
better for now. This tells me that we are going to be in power
for a long time … The world would end when Jesus comes.
That was the longest time I could think of.'[29]

'The media try to incite … I've also defended [the Afrikaans
song] De la Rey … I don't want war. I want peace … It's just
a nice song that people like. We used to sing it in the guerrilla
camps.'[30]

'The use of the word "appoint" in response to a question from
the media present was inadvertent and does not change the

28. 'JZ defends Shaik', *Independent on Saturday*, 14 March 2009. Zuma explaining
that the role of first lady would not be fulfilled by any one of his wives in
particular.

29. 'ANC backtracks on "ruling till Jesus comes"', *Business Day*, 3 April 2009. Zuma's
defence of his comments that the ANC would rule until Jesus returns, which
didn't amount to much; he would continue to use the phrase repeatedly.

30. Ibid. Zuma's defence of his singing of the song '*Awuleth' Umshini Wami*' ('Bring
me my machine').

fact I had decided merely to nominate Justice Ngcobo to this
position.'[31]

2010

'I have noted recent media reports about aspects of my
personal life. I have noted too that these reports have
been the subject of much discussion in the public arena by
various organisations and people from all walks of life. I
have therefore decided, after some careful deliberation, to
make public comment on a matter that is otherwise intensely
personal. I had been out of the country when this matter arose.
I confirm that I have a relationship and a baby with Sonono
Khoza.'[32]

'I have over the past week taken time to consider and reflect
on the issues relating to a relationship I had outside of
wedlock. The matter, though private, has been a subject of
much public discussion and debate. It has put a lot of pressure
on my family and my organisation, the African National
Congress. I also acknowledge and understand the reaction
of many South Africans. I deeply regret the pain that I have

---

31. Letter to the leaders of opposition parties, 19 August 2009. In an address to the
South African Press Association on 6 August, Zuma had said, 'I have decided to
nominate Justice Sandile Ngcobo as the next chief justice since Chief Justice
Pius Langa is due to retire.' Subsequent to his address, it was also reported that,
in explaining his choice, President Zuma stated that he had taken the decision
'properly' and 'objectively'. Importantly, it also reports the president as saying,
'The fact of the matter is that I have appointed a judge that I believe is capable.'
(*The Star*, independently of SAPA, also reports the president as saying this.) In
response to concern from opposition leaders, whom Zuma is constitutionally
obliged to consult on such matters, Zuma suggested that the error was a mere slip
of the tongue.

32. 'Statement by President Jacob Zuma on media reports about his child', 3 February
2010. After much speculation, Zuma would confirm that he had had an out-of-
wedlock relationship with Khoza and that he was the father of her child.

caused to my family, the ANC, the Alliance and South Africans in general.' [33]

2012

'They say I've said we did not care about the welfare of dogs. It's not true. I was saying we had love which took care and put everyone first and this love did not discriminate.' [34]

33. 'Media Statement: President Jacob Zuma's statement on the impact of events of the past week', 6 February 2010.

34. Speaking at a traditional cleansing ceremony in KwaZulu-Natal. 'Zuma calls for a national cleansing ceremony', SABC News, 28 December 2012. Zuma was addressing the outrage that had followed reports of his having said that white people cared more for their pets than for other people.

BETWEEN A ROCK AND A HARD PLACE

JACOB ZUMA AND THE MEDIA

*'If I were a journalist, I would write and say,
"The ANC is a wonderful organisation. It produces
wonderful leaders."'*

J acob Zuma believes that he in particular, and the ANC in general, has been done a great disservice by the South African media. The reasons for this are many and varied.

First, he believes the media is not 'transformed', in ANC parlance. In other words, it protects 'white' interests, is managed and controlled by 'white capital' and, as result, displays subtle racism in the stories it pursues. All of this, he believes, is to the detriment of the black majority and the vanguard of their interests, the ANC.

Second, he believes the media is not patriotic and, by implication, is treasonous in some way. This is not a flip-pant criticism. Any act of treason is a very serious crime indeed, punishable by death in some countries, yet the ANC often uses it in denigrating its opponents and crit-ics. This is because it sees the media as an illegitimate voice for public concern. As Zuma asked late in 2013, 'I've argued with them that they were never elected, we were elected and we can claim that we represent the people. They do say they represent the people. Does the population or public determine what is reported? They don't.'

The media, then, is a seen by the ANC and Zuma as an oppositional force, unelected and not representative of the will of the people, and often described in these terms. As a result, Zuma argues, there is much 'good news' that is not reported and the ANC government's performance is negatively targeted rather than positively celebrated. The government's 2014 slogan – 'we have a good story to tell' – was no doubt a response to this perceived constraint.

Third, that 'good story' is not simply substituted for an unpatriotic agenda by the media; in Zuma's mind it is subservient to sensationalism and ad hominem stories that play the man, not the ball. This is perhaps the only concern he shares with other political parties, and even some elements of the media itself. Zuma has often been unfairly targeted and, on numerous occasions, his privacy has indeed been violated. Thus, every now and then he speaks a hard truth. Nevertheless, he does not hesitate to pull out the victim card when rightly called out on some indiscretion, in the public interest.

The genesis of this hostility was Zuma's confrontation with the National Prosecuting Authority in 2003, when the director of public prosecutions at the time,

Bulelani Ngcuka, privately briefed black editors against Zuma. Later, Ngcuka said that the state had a prima facie case against Zuma but was not confident enough in its evidence to proceed to court. The NPA might have had a case, but its conduct suggested little more than a public smear campaign under the direction of Zuma's nemesis, former President Thabo Mbeki.

But Zuma's hostility towards the media was crystallised by his 2006 rape trial, a brutal political attempt at character assassination by his opponents. Zuma may have erred in his private affairs but the trial put his most personal life on public display. Between fair comment, he was ridiculed and lampooned from one front page to another. He was also found not guilty. His speech after the trial – directed at the media and quoted below – perhaps best defines the antagonism he has harboured towards the media ever since. That was Zuma at his angriest. The party's divisive 2007 elective conference, where he opposed and dethroned Mbeki, only reinforced this hostility, as he was viciously derided by many in the media who favoured his opponent.

The consequence of all of this is a perpetual war between Jacob Zuma and the fourth estate. He has tried to sue journalists for defamation on numerous occasions, but has rarely followed through all the way to court, which suggests a political purpose – intimidation, perhaps – rather than a defensible case. The cartoonist Zapiro has been his bête noire on this front. Other significant incidents (Brett Murray's *The Spear*, for example – a painting that portrayed Zuma in a Stalin-like pose with his private parts exposed, an image of which the *City Press* newspaper put online) redrew the battle lines. These were not only the lines between the ANC and the press, but also those between the ANC and the Constitution; for, ultimately, it is the right to freedom of expression that has been tested again and again under Zuma. That right might be battered and bruised but has remained intact.

The same attitude applies to the foreign media, with whom Zuma has had a similar experience.

It is ironic that, amid all of this supposedly unwarranted criticism, Zuma inherited the South African Broadcasting Corporation (SABC). This institution has become a metonym for the ANC's poor management of public institutions (it has been bailed out more times than one can count). In its supine attitude to the governing party, it has also come to represent just how much independent bodies have been politicised since 1994. The SABC's August 2013 announcement that it was striving for '70% good news' is testament to how deferential it is before the ANC's hegemonic agenda. One can be sure that the party approves of such an approach to objective news reporting.

Despite the national broadcaster's being in the ANC's pocket, it, too, has caused Zuma headaches. The politicisation of the institution worked against Zuma when he was first elected. He had many run-ins with the SABC, which would cut interviews and, Zuma argued, misrepresent him in news stories to portray him in a negative light. Then the ANC's programme of politicisation worked against Zuma. As he has done with so many other state institutions, he has since replaced those in the SABC who were loyal to Mbeki with those who are more eager to show the appropriate compliance before South Africa's new president.

Indeed, under Jacob Zuma, the ANC has taken its greatest strides since the advent of democracy towards facilitating a more government-friendly media. There was a time when Zuma and his party advocated starting their own newspaper, so desperate was the ANC for its story to be told. That soon gave way to a more lateral approach, but not before the ANC had tried a few other strategies.

First it tried the stick, threatening a media tribunal; then it turned to the carrot, and those sympathetic to the government of the day lined up to 'transform' the industry. Supplementing the SABC would be the advent of the satellite news channel ANN7, the establishment of *The New Age* newspaper and the February 2014 takeover of the Independent Group, all by people who have publicly dedicated themselves to telling the 'good news' story for which Zuma so often pines. However, the media houses and outlets not subject to this growing influence have not responded with sympathy – rather, with the righteous anger of a vital democratic mechanism under ever-increasing pressure. So, Zuma has alienated the media as much as he has transformed it.

Either way, Zuma's relationship to the media is central to understanding his personal narrative, as he feels the media is the primary obstacle to his establishing a credible reputation.

Zuma and the fourth estate

1999

'Another key issue for the media is whether they should
be taking party political stances. In the recent elections it
appeared that certain sections of the media expressed their
support for particular political parties and over certain
electoral campaign issues. We as a government cannot
prescribe the positions that the media takes on particular
issues. What we can say is that this is an issue the media
themselves must resolve. The danger, however, of the media
taking party political positions is that they become a player
in party politics.' [1]

2000

'For example, the media might transmit information of which
our enemies are unaware. It would then just be a simple
matter for our enemies to know what we were thinking and [to
formulate] plans to frustrate our plans.' [2]

2001

'We all agree that something has gone wrong in this country ...

---

1. Speech to the 1999 South African National Editors' Forum. 'Democracy challenge
to the media', *Cape Times*, 14 July 1999.

2. To a public seminar on intelligence oversight in the 21st century and in response
to criticism that, increasingly, intelligence portfolio committee hearings were
being held behind closed doors. 'Report carefully on SA intelligence, says Zuma',
Sowetan, 20 April 2000.

[I am concerned about television violence] that comes into our houses and the open sexual activities, like, for example, Big Brother.'[3]

2002

'I think that this Government, in itself, called for the independence of the SABC, if the hon member remembers – the ruling party in particular. That is why we have that independence. We cannot undermine it. I do not think there should be any worry about that. As the hon members know, it does not just come like a mushroom. It does not mushroom from the ground. There is a process which determines how the board comes about. There is an involvement of Government and there is a minister in charge. And, if there is a Minister in charge it means that independence is relative. It cannot be absolute. Therefore, the interaction between the Government and the SABC will always continue, otherwise what will the Minister be doing?'[4]

2003

'I assert that the NDPP [National Protector of Public Prosecutions] conducted the investigation in bad faith, motivated not by the need to earnestly search for the truth, but to cast aspersions on my integrity. An example of this is the manner in which detailed confidential information about the investigation was made readily available to certain sections of the media … The off-the-record briefing between the National

---

3. 'TV violence and sex come under attack', *Cape Argus*, 14 December 2001. In one of his more bizarre statements, Zuma would warn against the moral degeneration inherent to reality shows like *Big Brother*.

4. Answering questions in the National Assembly. Hansard, 11 September 2002, pp. 3280–3281.

Director and a select group of black editors in July this year also substantiates the view that the release of personal and confidential information about me to the media was part of a campaign aimed at destroying my reputation and to perpetuate mysterious agendas, rather than to further the course of justice ... This was definitely no ordinary media briefing; it was a character assassination exercise.'[5]

'I find it totally unacceptable and despicable that questions that they [the NPA] sent to me have appeared in a Sunday newspaper. This is a serious breach of confidentiality and is contrary to the spirit and terms of the National Prosecuting Authority Act, relating to the confidentiality of information received and disseminated.'[6]

2005

'The media acted as judges instead of reporting. It is an unfortunate situation. It has tried and sentenced Brett Kebble at great pain to his family, which was in grief.'[7]

---

5. In a press statement setting out a complaint laid by Zuma with the public protector against National Director of Public Prosecutions Bulelani Ngcuka, for a briefing with black editors on the case against Zuma as well as Ngcuka's statement that he believed that he had a 'prima facie' case against Zuma but refused to proceed with it. 'Zuma lodges complaint with protector against Ngcuka', South African Press Association, 7 November 2003. The public protector would later find that Ngcuka's actions 'unjustifiably infringed upon Mr Zuma's constitutional right to human dignity and caused him to be improperly prejudiced'.

6. Zuma responding to the decision by a newspaper to publish 35 questions sent to him by the NPA regarding his relationship with Schabir Shaik. 'Quoting the saga', *This Day*, 3 December 2003.

7. Addressing the South African Democratic Teachers Union Eastern Cape Congress. 'Zuma slams the media for trying both him and Kebble out of court', *Daily Dispatch*, 21 October 2005.

2006

'I said I did not do it [rape] and I am not guilty, but the media did something unusual. They tried me in a court of public opinion, and found me guilty. They tarnished my image. They swore at me and called me names. They did not wait for the court to find me guilty. They were not alone in this, but with political analysts. They called them to poke fun at me on television. Others did not do it intentionally but were sent by those hiding behind those who had ulterior motives. I kept my word – I wanted my day in court. They tried to confuse the nation and turn them against me. They were instructed by my enemies to spread nasty rumours.' [8]

'I have discovered the word "Zuma" on a front page sells. And I have seen some really bizarre headlines: "Zuma for Sale"; "Zuma's plan to hijack ANC"; "Zuma not a shoo-in"; "End of the road for Zuma"; "Zumania" and, amongst the most absurd, "Fear Factor – Bad Boy Zuma". Chasing sales and profits through unfair and sensational reporting compromises the individual's right to be treated with dignity and fairness.' [9]

'I believe that we will never truly know just how much that event altered the course of history of our country. Generally, we have a situation where some journalists have become

---

8. Zuma addressing a large crowd outside the courtroom after being acquitted on a rape charge. He was speaking in isiZulu and this is the translation. '"Media tarnished my image and swore at me"', *The Star*, 9 May 2006.

9. Speech to the 2006 South African National Editors' Forum Council. 'With freedom comes responsibility', 20 November 2006.

active participants in the events unfolding in the country. The end result is the blurring of the lines between fact and opinion.' [10]

2008

'The outcome of the 52nd national conference in Polokwane is a most recent example of the media yet again becoming a victim of its own propaganda and manipulation ... They indicate a general trend within most mainstream media institutions to adopt positions, cloaked as sober and impartial observation, that are antagonistic to the democratic movement and its agenda for fundamental social, political and economic transformation.' [11]

'[The media is] a product of the various political, social, economic and cultural forces within a society. It is a battle of ideas, and, as such, the media is part of the battle for power. Those with economic power are keen that the media serves to reinforce their privileged position, while those who seek a more equitable distribution of resources campaign for a media that serves the cause of a more equitable society ... At times, the media functions as if they are an opposition party.' [12]

'The media hype around an interview I had with the *Financial*

---

10. 'With freedom comes responsibility', 20 November 2006. The event to which Zuma referred was the briefing given by Director of Public Prosecutions Bulelani Ngcuka to black editors, against Zuma.

11. 'The voice of the ANC must be heard', *ANC Today* 8(2): 18–24, January 2008.

12. Ibid.

Times [UK], which reported that I said the president no longer
has any powers is mischievous. It is a misrepresentation of
what I said.' [13]

'We are destroying our society.' [14]

'While our media exists, it does not have space for the poor to
voice their views, hopes and dreams.' [15]

*'Koerante het nou al amper 15 jaar gehad om die publiek
in te lig. Hulle doen nie wat hulle sê nie. Ons waarneming
is dat hulle nie inlig oor vordering in die land nie. As
jy die kolomme en bladsye vat, is dit sensasioneel en nie
gebalanseerd nie. Lees jy wat slim mense van die media
skryf, wonder jy of dit die organisasie is waaraan jy
behoort. Koerante verdraai die waarheid en [sic] opskrifte.
Dit doen skade. Dit is onregverdige verslaggewing.'* [16]

---

13. 'Zuma denies everything', *The Times*, 11 March 2008. The *Financial Times* had
    reported Zuma as saying the following in a 6 March 2008 interview with the paper:
    'Power lies in the ANC. It's the ANC that wins elections, the ANC that has the
    power to identify people who must be part of government ... If he [the president]
    is not part of the ANC leadership, he doesn't have authority.'

14. A reference to the gratuitous display of sex and violence on television. 'We could
    have done more and we can still do more', *Sowetan*, 30 May 2008.

15. Speech to *Leadership* magazine's Tomorrow's Leaders Convention. 'Our South
    Africa', *Leadership*, 1 July 2008.

16. Said to the Free State ANC congress. 'Koerant vir ANC: Wat pla, vra Zuma', *Beeld*,
    26 July 2008. Zuma would probably have made the remark in English, but it was
    only reported in Afrikaans. The translation is: 'Newspapers have by now had
    almost 15 years to inform the public. Their actions do not reflect their words. Our
    observation is that they do not inform on progress in the country. If you look at
    the columns and pages, they are sensational and not balanced. When you read
    what the clever media people write, you wonder whether they are describing
    the organisation you belong to. Newspapers twist the truth in their headlines. It
    causes damage. It is unfair reporting.'

*'Die ANC het die leemte gesien, maar 'n besluit is nog nie
geneem nie. Ek sien dit nie as 'n misdaad nie. Die ANC
behoort nie vrae gevra word as hy dit doen nie. Enigiemand
het die reg om 'n koerant te begin. Hoekom moet die ANC nie
'n koerant begin om burgers behoorlik in te lig nie?'* [17]

'If I were a journalist, I would write and say, "The ANC is a
wonderful organisation. It produces wonderful leaders. There
is no organisation in the country that has produced leaders
like the ANC, arguably on this continent."' [18]

'I am not [*sic*] Jacob Zuma you have been reading about
because most media writers do not even know me.' [19]

2009

'If I were a journalist, I'd say that here in the southern tip
of Africa, you have a democracy that is rooted, which is
understood by the masses, a democracy in which no one
is above the law.' [20]

'The media is one institution that is extremely sensitive to
criticism, perhaps because practitioners spend their lives
criticizing other people. We do not only need to look at the

---

17. 'Koerant vir ANC: Wat pla, vra Zuma', *Beeld*, 26 July 2008. Zuma defending
the idea that the ANC should start its own newspaper to counter the negative
publicity it receives. The translation is: 'The ANC has seen the gap, but no
decision has been taken yet. I don't see it as a crime. The ANC should not be
questioned if it decides to do it. Anyone has the right to start a newspaper. Why
should the ANC not start a newspaper to inform our citizens properly?'

18. In an interview for *Leadership* magazine, in response to a question about whether
South Africans should be fearful of the change that might come with a Zuma
presidency. 'Zumafication of our nation, *Leadership*, 1 September 2008.

19. Ibid.

20. 'Jacob Zuma: a child of the ANC', *Sunday Independent*, 22 February 2009.

composition of newsrooms and ensure that they represent
the diversity of South African society. We also need to look at
the content of newsrooms, to ensure that they represent the
diversity of views and interests in our society.' [21]

'I don't know why we should not respect the privilege between
the doctor and the patient. Why, when the tests were done,
why was it published? Why did we bring the media in? We
must debate this issue. I don't think we are picking up the
issues that we ought to be picking up in respect to this young
girl; that we are in fact violating her rights.' [22]

2010

'These rights cannot be waived just because of a position one
occupies. I would request that the dignity and privacy of the
affected individuals in this matter be respected.' [23]

'It is unfortunate that the individuals concerned have been
unfairly subjected to harsh media exposure merely because
of the position that I occupy. Our constitution and our laws
require us to protect children from harmful public exposure.
The constitution states that it is inappropriate to place at risk

---

21. Speech, commemorating Nat Nakasa, to the 2009 South African National Editors'
    Forum, 30 June 2009.

22. In response to an enquiry from a journalist at a press conference after the second
    South Africa–European Union summit. 'Zuma chastises media for having lack of
    respect', *Saturday Star*, 12 September 2009. Following Caster Semenya's victory
    at the 2009 World Championships, she had been subjected to gender testing, the
    results of which were made public, generating a huge outcry. Zuma no doubt
    related powerfully to the violation of her privacy and her humiliation. This was
    his response.

23. 'Statement by President Jacob Zuma on media reports about his child', 3 February
    2010. After much speculation, Zuma would confirm that he had had an out-of-
    wedlock relationship with Sonono Khoza and that he was the father of her child.

the child's wellbeing, physical or mental health, and spiritual, moral or social development.' [24]

'The media is also in essence questioning the right of the child to exist and, fundamentally, her right to life. It is unfortunate that the matter has been handled in this way. I sincerely hope the media will protect the rights of children.' [25]

'When the British came to our country, they said everything we are doing was barbaric, was wrong, inferior in whatever way. Bear in mind that I am a freedom fighter and I fought to free myself, also for my culture to be respected. And I don't know why they are continuing thinking that their culture is more superior than others, those who might have said so. I am very clear on these issues, I've not looked down upon any cultures of anyone … and no one has been given authority to judge others. The British have done that before, as they colonised us, and they continue to do this, and it's an unfortunate thing. If people want an engagement, I'm sure we will engage on that issue.' [26]

2013

'When I go out, people envy South Africans, they wish they were South Africans because they say we are doing so well, we are succeeding … they love it. But when I am in South Africa, every

---

24. 'Statement by President Jacob Zuma on media reports about his child', 3 February 2010

25. Ibid.

26. '"Buffoon" Zuma hits back', *The Star*, 3 March 2010. Ahead of an official state visit to the United Kingdom, his first major international country visit, Zuma was savaged in the British press, particularly, by the *Daily Mail*, which described Zuma and his polygamy as a 'buffoon' and a 'sex-obsessed bigot'. Others called him 'barbaric' and 'inferior'. They focused, too, on his out-of-wedlock child with Sonono Khoza. This was Zuma's response.

morning you feel like you must leave this country because the
reporting concentrates on the opposite of the positive.'[27]

'Why don't I read about this [crime] in the media, because in
my country, you read about everything.'[28]

'Patriotic reporting.'[29]

'I've argued with them that they were never elected, we were
elected and we can claim that we represent the people. They
do say they represent the people. Does the population or
public determine what is reported? They don't.'[30]

'The coverage of news in a more patriotic manner does not
mean that journalists should not report in an objective and
balanced manner. It means ensuring balance and fairness and
putting the country first before any other consideration.'[31]

---

27. Addressing journalism students from the Tshwane University of Technology
    who were visiting Parliament as part of a trip to Cape Town. 'Zuma condemns
    "opposite of the positive" SA media', *Mail & Guardian*, 10 September 2013. One
    of many criticisms levelled at the media by Zuma and the ANC, in which they are
    argue that the press does not report the real South African story.

28. 'Zuma condemns "opposite of the positive" SA media'. Here Zuma was
    referencing Mexico, where he said, upon visiting, that he was struck by how
    patriotic journalists in that country did not run the country down by reporting bad
    news about crime.

29. Ibid. To illustrate his point, Zuma used the example of Mexico, which he said
    practised 'patriotic reporting', in which negative news stories, particularly about
    crime, were effectively suppressed by journalists themselves, for the national good.

30. Ibid. Zuma has often argued that the press is not a legitimate voice of public
    sentiment because its members were not elected.

31. 'Zuma calls on media to "put the country first"', *The Times*, 29 October 2013.
    Zuma, elaborating on a reply to a Parliamentary question about his earlier
    comments on news reporting in Mexico. For more, see 'Replies to Parliamentary
    Questions for Written Reply', The Presidency, Internal Question Paper No. 31 of
    2013, 29 October 2013. Zuma tries to have his cake and eat it here. One cannot
    demand balance and fairness, and that patriotism be put 'before every other
    consideration', mainly because there is no agreement on what patriotism is when
    it comes to news.

2014

'I used to practise witchcraft around here, bewitching the Boers during apartheid.' [32]

'We need a media sector that is an accurate mirror of ourselves regardless of race, colour, gender, class, creed or geographical location. A media sector that will tell the full South African story, and balance the challenges we face of unemployment, inequality and poverty, with the remarkable achievements that the country has also scored. Very few countries have emerged from conflict and managed to build a thriving democracy, achieve peace and stability, fully functional democratic institutions and to build a new nation as we have done as South Africans, in a short space of time. If we do not tell this story ourselves, and instead choose to be overly-critical and paint a wrong picture that our country is failing when it is not, we are doing South Africa and South Africans who work hard, a huge disservice.' [33]

---

32. 'South African president Zuma reveals he used to practice witchcraft against white people', *Daily Mail*, 9 January 2014. In a story that relied more on sensation than salience, the *Daily Mail* used this quote to paint Zuma as having a 'voodoo past'. A furious response from Mac Maharaj, spokesperson for the president, said: 'It appears that some journalists, who probably do not understand the isiZulu language, did a literal translation and lost the meaning'. He called the story 'ridiculous and misleading'. See 'Media Statement: Witchcraft reports are ridiculous', 10 January 2014.

33. Speech at the launch of Independent Newspapers and Media SA under new ownership, Cape Town, 28 February 2014. The sale of the Independent Group to the Sekunjalo consortium was widely criticised as a move to introduce a 'government-friendly' approach to news reporting into the organisation, one complemented by the advent of the *New Age* newspaper and the Gupta-family-owned ANN7 television news channel. In welcoming ANN7, the ANC said that 'the South African story remains largely untold'.

Zuma versus Zapiro

If there is one person who has come to epitomise Zuma's hostile relationship with the media, it is cartoonist Jonathan Shapiro, better known as Zapiro. He has, in many different cartoons, brutally mocked the president. He now routinely draws a shower protruding from the top of Zuma's head (a reference to his rape trial remark that he had a shower after sex to minimise the risk of contracting HIV/Aids) and, most notoriously, drew a cartoon of Lady Justice held spreadeagled on the floor by Zuma's associates, with him poised above, seemingly ready to rape her.

Zuma lodged a R5-million defamation case, later reduced to R100 000, against Zapiro. He eventually withdrew it, ostensibly because he claimed it was a distraction but in reality because he stood no real chance of winning it or because he would have been required to testify – which would have opened the door to his every action concerning South Africa's justice system being cross-examined under oath in the High Court, something that would probably have further damaged, rather than enhanced, his reputation.

Zapiro has had to face other legal challenges from Zuma. He was originally sued for R15 million (part of a bigger R63-million claim) for three cartoons published by Independent Newspapers – Zuma being sworn in as president in court; a depiction of Zuma and the moral degeneration handbook; and his first cartoon of Zuma with a shower protruding from his head.

2010

'Such claims will have the effect of restricting freedom of expression and commentary on matters of public interest.' [34]

'Although the SAHRC finds the cartoon and the words used in relation thereto probably offensive and distasteful, same falls short of and does not constitute hate speech, unfair discrimination under Promotion of Equality and the Prevention of Unfair Discrimination Act or a violation of any fundamental human right contained in the Constitution.' [35]

2012

'We find it unacceptable and shocking that after the harsh experiences that South Africa, the president and his family has experienced few weeks ago, that Zapiro and the Mail and Guardian will find it appropriate to continue with the insults and hurt to the president, his family and the broader ANC constituency ... We believe we are not alone as the ANC in

---

34. 'Media Statement: Sanef shocked at defamation claim by President Zuma against *Sunday Times*', South African National Editors' Forum, 19 December 2010. In reaction to the defamation action instituted by President Jacob Zuma against Avusa, the *Sunday Times*, its editor-in-chief Mondli Makhanya and Jonathan Shapiro over the Lady Justice cartoon that had been published in the *Sunday Times* over two years earlier.

35. 'Finding in the matter between Manamela, Buti and Others (Complainant) and Shapiro, Jonathan (Respondent)', South African Human Rights Commission, Case Reference No. GP/2008/1037/E MOKONYAMA, 12 May 2010.

condemning this act of insult to our President by Zapiro and the Mail and Guardian, all South Africans share our disgust.'[36]

'The furore created by "The Spear" is a clear indication that we still have a long way to go. The Zapiro cartoons rely on their shock value to make an impact, but by calling the President of this great nation a "dick" is unacceptable and the WL would like to know who the "we" he is referring to in the cartoon actually is, as the majority of the population who voted for the President clearly did not think this of Zuma. This cartoon is a clear attempt to fuel divisions in our society and should be condemned by all proud South Africans, regardless of race or political affiliation.'[37]

'It is mindboggling that a cartoonist of his stature seeks to portray himself as a victim.'[38]

'After careful consideration and consultation with his legal team, President Zuma has taken a decision to withdraw his claim against the respondents, and pay a contribution to their costs.'[39]

---

36. ANC national spokesperson Jackson Mthembu. 'Media Statement: ANC condemns the cartoon by Zapiro and the Mail and Guardian Newspaper', 6 July 2012. This time the cartoon depicted Zuma as a penis, and featured a pen that referred to him as a 'dick'.

37. ANC Women's League spokeswoman Troy Martens in response to the Zapiro 'penis' cartoon. 'Media Statement: ANCWL Condemns lastest [sic] Zapiro Excuse for Satire', 6 July 2012.

38. 'Cartoonist plays victim – Maharaj', The Citizen, 4 September 2012.

39. Spokesperson for the presidency, Mac Maharaj. 'Media Statement: President Zuma withdraws case against Mr Shapiro and Avusa', 28 October 2012. Explaining Zuma's decision to withdraw his R5-million claim against Zapiro.

'Whereas the President believes that in an open and democratic society, a fine and sensitive balance needs to be maintained between the exercise of civil rights such as freedom of speech, and the dignity and privacy of others, that balance should be struck in favour of constitutional freedoms. The President therefore would like to avoid setting a legal precedent that may have the effect of limiting the public exercise of free speech, with the unforeseen consequences this may have on our media, public commentators and citizens.' [40]

'I think the ANC has been shockingly thin-skinned. I have been very, very disappointed in many ANC people and government people. It is because of the ANC's struggle and certain individuals that we have the freedoms that we have [and] the constitution. Now that they are being put under scrutiny and are being shown sometimes to be corrupt, they are now trying to roll back the freedoms they helped bring about.' [41]

---

40. 'Media Statement. Presient Zuma withdraws case against Mr Shapiro and Avusa', 28 October 2012.

41. Jonathan Shapiro, defending his cartooning after an attack on him by spokesperson for the Presidency, Mac Maharaj, in an interview on 567 CapeTalk/ Radio 702. 'Mac, Zapiro trade blows', *The Times*, 30 October 2012. Maharaj had said, among other things, 'I've not called him a racist, I'm saying there are issues of prejudice in our country, and that particular cartoon illustrates that problem.'

THE PURSUIT OF POWER: LOYALTY AND BETRAYAL

JACOB ZUMA AND HIS RISE TO POWER

'I do not get angry. Perhaps that is why the ANC
made me the chief of intelligence.'

Jacob Zuma has friends and enemies in equal measure. Some of his friends became his enemies, just as some of his enemies became his friends. Thus, he has enjoyed great loyalty and suffered significant betrayal. One might say that this is typical of any politician, but what differentiates Zuma is the informal patronage network he has established around himself – his friends and enemies are often a consequence of his proximity to power and he structures those relationships more as a tribal chief than a president. The result is a patriarch who sits atop a powerful, patronage-based, unofficial system of political influence that has little to do with his constitutional authority and everything to do with the sort of off-the-record access he can provide to it.

To understand the unofficial rules that govern these sorts of relationships, one must understand demagoguery. It is a contradiction of sorts – the utilitarian impulse to please the greatest number of people as often as possible combined with the selfish desire to be the primary beneficiary of the resultant affirmation or praise. Thus, principles are sacrificed in the name of expediency. When it comes to friendship, anyone can qualify. And Zuma has the personality to make that possible: he exudes charm and charisma in embracing all who come into his circle.

From Helen Zille, his main political opponent outside those in the ANC, to civil society, through to his adversaries in the media, everyone will tell you that it is very difficult not to like him after a one-on-one conversation.

However, if Zuma's friends are not demagogues themselves, they will inevitably wonder what, if anything, they have in common with his other acquaintances. When Zuma disagrees with some in his circle and his response to that conflict is appeasement, the first question that those who are forced to watch will be left to ponder is, 'Does he care more about my interests or the interests of my enemy?' Often they are disappointed with the answer. And, if the answer is indeed the latter, the friendship fails. That is the cost of trying to accommodate allcomers.

The price, then, of being a demagogue is suffering love and hate to the same degree. Demagogues' enemies loathe them as much as their friends like them. Once one has fallen outside that informal network, the only way back in is through deference. Come bearing gifts, and one shall have a seat at the table. Dislike the other guests, and one shall be removed. Once shunned, it is possible to see that the emperor is wearing no clothes, but by then it is too late. So, any demagogue is by nature divisive.

Brett Murray's *The Spear*, is a metaphor for Zuma in more ways than one. In a country where poor education levels make the visual image far more powerful than the written word, *The Spear* cut to Zuma's very heart.

Once, Zuma could count amongst his friends President Thabo Mbeki, ANC Youth League President Julius Malema and Cosatu Secretary General Zwelinzima Vavi. Now, these three very powerful people are his enemies, all having been systematically frozen out of the ANC and from access to Jacob Zuma. Some were willing to indulge Zuma when he was not a threat. Others were willing to die for Zuma, when he served their interests. But all of them, at some point, saw or experienced Zuma for what he was: a mirror that reflected whoever was looking into it. And, when they weren't looking into this mirror themselves, they saw in Zuma their enemies – and their enemies' policies.

Julius Malema best represents this sort of fundamental change but one should not forget how loyal Zuma was to former President Mbeki. Often he put his own reputation on the line to defend his leader. At the height of the Mbeki HIV/Aids controversy, Zuma described the president as 'towering'. Zuma must have felt betrayed when Mbeki, with every state apparatus he could muster, turned on him.

Along the way he has been forced to face other obstacles – ethnic and tribal squabbling, factionalism, infighting, even breakaway parties. He has dismissed or downplayed them all as insignificant and, in doing so, always refers to the abstract ideal as opposed to the practical reality.

Through it all, Zuma endured. The ANC's policy of cadre deployment has saved Zuma many times – not just by engendering a culture of deference to the party's internal hierarchy and consequent subservience to the revolutionary project, allowing many to be redeployed without resistance, but by his being so effacing before it himself that he has sought to create the impression that he is a mere loyal and humble servant to the cause, without ambition or personal desire. For someone with no aspiration, and without real vision or purpose, he certainly has come far. He keeps his hands clean for the most part, rarely denigrating an opponent publicly, and lets his internal politicking deliver whatever message he has for his adversaries.

All of this suggests a man who is brutally calculating,

with a personal demeanour that is inauthentic and self-serving. This is only half-true. Zuma understands very well the rules of engagement; in private, he executes them with ruthless efficiency. He has spared few in ensuring that his own position is consolidated and protected, but this does not mean that his natural impulse is not to befriend. Whether Zuma has many real friends – the kind he would have made had he never entered politics – is difficult to know. No doubt there are some. They must watch his expanding and contracting circle of acquaintances with bemusement.

Zuma, friends and enemies

1997

'One would think that the ANC is involved in a process foreign to other political parties. Is it not every party's right to decide which cadres to deploy and also conduct rearrangements should the need arise? I do not sit in my office and plot my next move. We do not do that in the ANC culture and are certainly not at war as some may so desperately like to believe. We get deployed.'[1]

'Nobody is anybody's person in the ANC. People at times miss the fact that there are comprehensive internal debates in the ANC, and when the media picks up aspects of the debate it says there is a problem. It is those debates that make the ANC strong … Nobody cannot express a view, but the correct argument wins the day. I have not seen any cabals.'[2]

'As a collective, the ANC identifies a task that needs to be performed and then deploys a suitable person for that

---

1. 'Staying out of the election bun-fight', *Pretoria News*, 3 November 1997.

2. In an interview, in response to the suggestion that Thabo Mbeki led a cabal that 'takes all the decisions and sidelines or destroys the political careers of those outside the circle'. 'The ANC's ready for a mega-mission', *Sunday Times*, 2 November 1997. In the run-up to the ANC's 1997 Mafikeng conference, where Zuma would be elected ANC deputy president, eventually beating Winnie Madikizela-Mandela, he spent much of November conducting interviews with the press in which he did two things: suggest he had no personal ambition, and reinforce and defend his relationship with Thabo Mbeki, who would be elected president. Later (see note 4), he would be accused of being 'too close' to Mbeki.

particular task. A disciplined cadre of the movement will abide by the decision.'[3]

'I've worked with Thabo just as I've worked with others in the ANC. Why do they say I am close to Steve Tshwete with whom I shared a prison cell and was together in exile? It so happens that I have worked with Thabo and that his approach to issues is very close to mine. We have a similar political understanding.'[4]

2000

'In our view, our President today is towering. He is, in fact, at the level of presidents in the developed countries. He has brought innovation in the debates that have taken place.'[5]

'I do not know what damage the President has caused. What I know is that the President asked specific questions which were aimed at getting information from those who know, particularly scientists, so that Government could take

---

3. 'The ANC's ready for a mega-mission', *Sunday Times*, 2 November 1997.

4. In response to the suggestion that he was too close to Mbeki. He was described as 'irritated' by the question. 'Zuma an "old-school" ANC cadre', *City Press*, 23 November 1997.

5. Answering questions in the National Assembly. Hansard, 7 June 2000, p. 2129. Zuma was asked about President Thabo Mbeki's lack of credibility, in particular on Zimbabwe and in light of the ANC's policy of quiet diplomacy.

informed positions as it works out its policies to deal with this matter.'[6]

2001

'I have no intention of standing for the presidency of the party next year because we have a president who is doing very well.'[7]

2003

'I have led by example since I came to the leadership in any capacity and I am still leading by example.'[8]

2005

'In ANC culture we do not put our names forward, we do not tout ourselves. It is the ANC that decides who should lead the party. Once ANC members reach an agreement, they then

---

6. Answering questions in the National Assembly. Hansard, 1 November 2000, pp. 4328–4329. On 4 May 2000, the full Presidential Advisory Panel on AIDS was announced by the Minister of Health. It was made up of 33 HIV/Aids 'experts' from around the world and was roughly divided between 'orthodox' scientists who believe that the collection of symptoms known as Aids is caused by the virus known as HIV, and the 'dissidents', who believe, to varying degrees, that Aids doesn't exist, that HIV doesn't cause Aids or that Aids is caused by lifestyle factors like drugs, homosexuality or poverty. On 11 September 2000, Mbeki told *Time* magazine that '… the notion that immune deficiency is only acquired from a single virus cannot be sustained'. And, on 20 September, Mbeki told Parliament that '[w]e need to look at the question that is posed, understandably I suppose: does HIV cause AIDS? AIDS the acronym stands for Acquired Immune Deficiency Syndrome. Now I do believe that is a sensible thing to ask: does one virus cause a syndrome? A virus cannot cause a syndrome. A virus will cause a disease'.

7. 'ANC's heir apparent speaks from the heart', *Sowetan*, 6 June 2001. Mbeki was in the midst of his HIV/Aids controversy at the time.

8. Answering questions in the National Assembly. In response to a question about whether his credibility as the head of South Africa's moral regeneration movement had suffered in light of the corruption allegations that hung over his head. 'I won't quit says unrepentant Zuma', *Eastern Province Herald*, 10 September 2003.

approach you and say they want to nominate you. It is at that point you can either accept or decline. You don't go round saying, "I want to be the president".' [9]

'He is more than a comrade, he is my brother. We have been together and we share views – we are much closer than people think.' [10]

'We have worked together for over 30 years very closely and in government. I still hold him in high esteem. My comradeship will continue. He is president of the ANC and I am the deputy president of the ANC. We sit together every Monday in the same meeting.' [11]

2006

'This is not a Xhosa/Zulu issue. As one of the leaders of the ANC I have support across the country. Otherwise I wouldn't have been elected into many leadership positions, including that of being the deputy president. It was not Zulus who were electing me, I was elected by people from across the board. The unfortunate thing is that, in politics, people love to use labels to further their own desires. The truth is that wherever I go, be it Limpopo or Eastern Cape, I get the same reception that I get in KZN.' [12]

---

9. In response to the interview question, 'Do you want to be president of South Africa?' '"In ANC you don't say: I want to be president"', *Mail & Guardian*, 12 May 2005.

10. Ibid. In response to the question, 'How is your relationship with president Mbeki?'

11. On his relationship with Thabo Mbeki. 'Why I would not quit', *Sunday Independent*, 19 June 2005.

12. 'I'm popular all over – Zuma', *The Star*, 16 January 2006. Zuma had recently been removed from the position of deputy president at the time by Thabo Mbeki, following his rape accusation. He was dismissing the rumour that there were ethnic forces at play.

'I do not bear grudges for other people. I do not get
angry. Perhaps that is why the ANC made me the chief
of intelligence.'[13]

'I don't jump up if someone tells a lie about me. You can't be
chasing shadows, otherwise you'll turn round until you fall
down with dizziness. I have been taught by the ANC that you
must understand and differentiate between your enemies
and your comrades. Enemies come in many forms – there are
some who are pronounced and open, there are some who are
secretive. So I always say the truth will triumph, time will tell.
Time is the biggest answer to many things.'[14]

'I really would not like to enter into a debate with the
Archbishop. I respect the Archbishop and his views. However,
there is no such thing as the presidential race in the ANC.
Therefore it is not correct for the Archbishop to say I should
pull out of the race. Which race?'[15]

2008

'Power lies in the ANC … It's the ANC that wins elections, the
ANC that has the power to identify people who must be part
of government … If he [the president] is not part of the ANC

---

13. '"If I was guilty I wouldn't be so strong"', *The Star*, 17 January 2006. Also in
    response to his firing as deputy president.

14. 'Truth will always triumph, says Zuma', *Daily Dispatch*, 19 July 2006.

15. In response to a call from Archbishop Desmond Tutu, a long-time adversary and
    critic of Zuma, for Zuma to abandon his presidential ambitions. 'I'm in no race,
    says Zuma', *The Citizen*, 23 September 2006.

leadership, he doesn't have authority.' [16]

'Mbeki is president of the republic; Zuma is president of the ANC. There are no to centres of power. Mbeki has to undertake specific tasks as state president, but he gets his mandate from the ANC. There is one centre and that is [in the party].' [17]

'That is why we have taken these measures to ensure that the ANC in the Western Cape is properly geared to deal with the challenges of elections. It is that part that would have informed the decision that has been taken.' [18]

'Once you allow that tendency [of centralising power] you are in danger that the people will not be able to defend their democracy [or] defend their power. And I've been warning [that] we should be wary of this, we must never allow it. It is a dangerous thing.' [19]

'I would prefer to leave after one term … Even if it is not one term, I think in the second term I should be able to … begin the process of winding down. I would allow open debate,

---

16. Interview with British newspaper the *Financial Times*. 'Zuma says he is more powerful than Mbeki', *Financial Times*, 6 March 2008. This comment would cause Zuma no end of grief and he would later state that it was taken out of context and misrepresented, and that any pretence that he was demeaning Mbeki was 'mischievous'.

17. 'Trust the ANC to choose the right man to lead the country, says party chief', *Sowetan*, 29 May 2008.

18. 'Rasool's removal part of plan to win W Cape', *The Star*, 24 July 2008. Zuma explaining his reasoning for removing former Western Cape Premier Ebrahim Rasool from his position.

19. '"I want only one term"', *Sunday Argus*, 27 July 2008. Zuma said the Polokwane conference had been 'a lesson to the ANC'.

not make people guess what is going to happen in terms of succession. This would allow the organization to indicate what it wants. But if it was me deciding, if the ANC had made me president of the country [I would prefer one term].'[20]

'I was deputy secretary-general, I was national chairperson and I was deputy president. All the time, I have been number two to Mbeki. Now for somebody to close their eyes and say, "Now there is a new president of the ANC and therefore there is a totally new leadership with new policies on the way", that person does not understand the internal workings of the ANC.'[21]

'I think he is going to grow within the ANC leadership and appreciate and learn from that leadership around him. As an uneducated man myself, I understand that sometimes the figures of speech we use in English are taken literally instead of figuratively and people took him to task on what he said. Instead of helping the young man, we make such a big hullabaloo about it. Let the young man grow, please, his potential is big and his heart is in the right place. The young people have felt he should be there and because they think they need that kind of leader at this time.'[22]

---

20. "'I want only one term"', *Sunday Argus*, 27 July 2008. A key Zuma quote, unfortunately replete with incomplete phrases and sentences, which is quoted as it appeared in the newspaper. It is nevertheless telling enough, and certainly there has been precious little evidence of this personal desire. Indeed, in the midst of his Nkandla controversy and with the 2014 elections looming, Zuma said that he would 'never' resign, '[b]ecause I think I have got a commitment that I made, firstly to liberate South Africa, secondly to change the quality of life of this country. As long as the ANC gives me that opportunity I can't say halfway [I'll resign], as if I decided on my own. I didn't apply for this job, I was deployed to do the job.' Interview with eNCA, 16 February 2014.

21. 'Zumafication of our nation', *Leadership*, 1 September 2008.

22. Ibid. On Julius Malema and his future potential.

'I may be different to Thabo Mbeki, who is more economically inclined, a bit forceful, impatient with slow-thinkers and argumentative. I am different to Mandela, who is very patient, but very expressive in getting his point across when it matters. I like discussing and debating with people and I like people to be aware of what is happening. I believe mostly in the collective and collective leadership.' [23]

'This time in particular you have an opportunity that as people say there is an administration coming to an end, so if you do so, *unjengomuntu oshaya inyoka esifile uyayishaya inyoka ife kudala, uyayishaya kodwa* wasting energy. [It's like a person who keeps hitting a snake once it is dead. The snake is dead so it's just redundant to keep hitting it. The snake is dead but the person is still beating it.]' [24]

'The National Executive Committee of the ANC met over the weekend of the 19th to 21st September 2008, to deliberate on various pertinent issues. After careful debate and discussion the NEC decided to recall Comrade Thabo Mbeki. This was one of the most difficult decisions the NEC has ever had to take in the history of the ANC.' [25]

---

23. 'Zumafication of our nation', *Leadership*, 1 September 2008.

24. Addressing a crowd of ANC supporters at the Pretoria Showgrounds. 'Attacking Mbeki govt "like beating a dead snake" – Zuma', South African Press Association, 14 September 2008. Mbeki had just had the Nicholson judgment handed down against him, which found the decision to pursue charges against Zuma unlawful. Nicholson's judgment was later unanimously overturned by the Supreme Court of Appeal.

25. 'Media Statement: Recall of the President of the Republic: Statement by the President of the African National Congress, Jacob Zuma on behalf of the ANC National Executive Committee', 22 September 2008. Zuma would make the official announcement, but it was ANC Secretary General Gwede Mantashe who would have the task of telling Mbeki personally.

'Everything is under control. There must be no panic. There is a tendency among people who analyse to exaggerate things. There is absolutely no constitutional crisis. Their analysis would be correct if things were not done under the parameters of the law and if people were forced to leave.' [26]

'I think Zuma is hated so much. It comes out very clearly.' [27]

'It was not how the government was doing, it was a different matter. It was different issues that related to that matter. It was never that he failed as head of government. That's why I quote him … I am saying, not that he failed to advance the programme of the ANC; there were other matters that related to government that people had a problem with, which caused quite serious problems in the ANC.' [28]

2009

'We have no doubt that Mr Cele will lead the SAPS efficiently

---

26. To journalists at the annual King Shaka Day celebrations held in KwaDukuza, in response to the ANC's decision to recall President Thabo Mbeki, just four days earlier. 'Zuma mum on new cabinet', South African Press Association, 24 September 2008. Zuma had known what he was talking about ten days earlier, when he had said that the Mbeki administration was a 'dead snake'. It was now truly buried.

27. Explaining that the newly formed Congress of the People (COPE) was founded on hate for certain individuals in the ANC. 'Why do you hate me so much', *City Press*, 9 November 2008. Zuma suggested that after those who had formed COPE were voted out of the ANC, 'that's when they started analyzing individuals and [saying] the ANC is going to be this and is going to be that'.

28. Ibid. On why he recalled President Mbeki from government. Odd reasoning, given that Mbeki was an elected official. Later Zuma would say 'No, not at all' when asked if he would like to elaborate on his reasoning.

and effectively.' [29]

'The ANC recognizes talent and leadership and we give people an opportunity. Julius has illustrated that he is indeed a good leader and that he understands people.' [30]

2010

'I deal with ministers properly. In cabinet we also deal with such matters. Although it's not been the order of the day, I don't think it will ever happen again. I absolutely read the riot act. That's why you can't see them continuing fighting.' [31]

2011

'I have also decided to suspend the National Commissioner from duty with immediate effect, pending the outcome of the inquiry, in terms of section 8(3)(a) read with Section 9(1) of

---

29. Statement on his decision to appoint Bheki Cele, a long-time ally, as the new South African Police Services Commissioner. 'Media Statement: Announcement by South African President Jacob Zuma of new National Police Commissioner', 29 July 2009. Cele's appointment was widely criticised as the president rewarding loyalty rather than expertise. Zuma eventually fired Cele, after he was found to have acted irregularly in the awarding of an SAPS lease agreement by the public protector. Cele took Zuma to court to have the decision overturned. His founding affidavit accused the president of never providing an explanation for his dismissal.

30. 'Shock at Zuma's Malema remark', *Sowetan*, 27 October 2009. The *Sowetan* framed Zuma's comments as an indication from the president that he regarded Malema as 'worthy of being the country's president in future', but Zuma did not, in fact, use that phrase. Nevertheless, that became the debate, with a number of newspaper editorials decrying Zuma's lack of judgement.

31. In an interview with the *Sunday Times* in response to a question about public bickering between members of his cabinet. 'I am decisive', *Sunday Times*, 21 February 2010.

the South African Police Service Act.' [32]

2012

'We will especially miss his energy, as he was a remarkably hard worker, and his impact was greatly felt in the local government turnaround strategy, as well as his contribution to the struggle from the early 1980s.' [33]

'If you have a fellow like Malema, first you have got to understand him. And if you understand Malema you know how to handle Malema. If you don't understand him you will never be able to handle him.' [34]

'I think the objective is how do you help Malema – because Malema has a lot of elements that are good in him. At one point I said there is a lot of potential in this young man. What you have got to do is deal with things that are not right with Malema. I don't think you should have an objective to remove him. We must help him to do the right things. Because if you help him to do the right things you have a very good potential young man who could put across things very well. But you

---

32. 'Media Statement: Special announcements by President Zuma', 24 October 2011. After much procrastination, Zuma suspended Bheki Cele before firing him. He cleverly couched the announcement in a wide-ranging set of changes to his cabinet, diverting some attention from it.

33. At the funeral for late Minister of Co-operative Governance Sicelo Shiceka. 'Tributes pour in for former minister', *Cape Times*, 1 May 2012. Zuma had fired the minister after the public protector found him to have 'deliberately and inadvertently misled the President when he presented the purpose of his visit to Switzerland', to have 'travelled to Switzerland under false pretenses and at state expense', and to have shown conduct that was 'not in the best interest of good governance, not performed in good faith and inconsistent with the integrity of his office and of the Government'.

34. 'Trust and respect goes both ways – Zuma', *The Star*, 10 May 2012. In response to the question, 'How is this [Malema] being handled by you as a leader?'

cannot allow him to do the wrong things. In other words, the
job of the ANC is to help Malema, to mold him into a dynamic,
good leader. That's what we need to do. It is only if you can't
do that the question becomes what do we do with him. Now
the ANC never give [*sic*] up on people. It has patience. I think
what we should do is help Malema.' [35]

'You know you can live with a snake, but you must know
whether it has teeth or it doesn't, whether it is poisonous or
not. If it is not poisonous, no fangs, you can play around with
it. If it is poisonous and has fangs, you must learn how to live
with it. Keep it at arm's length. But understand what type of a
snake, is it dangerous or not?' [36]

'… dishonesty, vague answers and a conflict of interest.' [37]

'I don't feel much because to me it has exposed what type
of a person he is, it has exposed the depth of his politics,
it has exposed to me the level of his care and love of the
organisation. When he says he loves it, anyone who loves this
organisation does not behave like that. I don't think I've got

---

35. 'Trust and respect goes both ways – Zuma'. In response to the question, 'Of
course some detractors may ask, what is the prospect of removing Malema from
public space once and for all?' Malema had already been expelled from the party,
in November 2011, for provoking divisions and bringing the organisation into
disrepute. At the time of this interview he had lost his final appeal to have the
decision overturned (in April 2012), so quite how Zuma expected the party to help
Malema is difficult to understand. From this point onwards, Malema set his sights
on opposing the ANC at the polls.

36. Addressing delegates at the SACP's congress at the University of Zululand.
'Beware the snakes among us – Zuma', *City Press*, 13 July 2012. Zuma was
warning against dangerous members inside the ANC

37. Replying affidavit by Jacob Zuma, in response to former Police Commissioner
Bheki Cele challenging the president's decision to fire him. 'Why I sacked Cele –
Zuma', *City Press*, 30 September 2012.

time to waste on such matters really.' [38]

2013

'The new members will be sworn in tomorrow. Thank you very much and goodbye.' [39]

'People are asking why she was not axed. They don't understand her duties and responsibilities. I am satisfied about what she is doing because she knows her work very well. Even on the issue of Limpopo textbooks … people who don't know says [sic] she was supposed to have delivered textbooks. People must understand that there are national and provincial responsibilities and duties, and delivering books is a provincial responsibility.' [40]

'I cannot talk in public why I have appointed so and so, and why I had changed so and so. They are my colleagues

38. 'Jacob Zuma says Marikana killings a wake-up call on workers' conditions', *The Guardian* (UK), 13 December 2012. In a wide-ranging interview, when asked about Julius Malema's expulsion from the ANC and criticisms of himself.

39. Concluding the announcement of his sixth cabinet reshuffle in five years. 'Zuma wields axe again', *The Star*, 10 July 2013. Zuma offered no explanation of his changes, which included the axing of compromised communications minister Dina Pule. At the time of writing, he had made 61 changes to his executive (ministers and deputy ministers) since 2009. A total of 114 different directors general have served in either permanent or acting capacities since President Zuma first came to office in May 2009. In that time, the average lifespan of a director general was just 15 months or 450 days.

40. In an interview with Durban-based radio station Gagasi FM, quoted in 'Angie Motshekga is doing an "excellent" job, says Zuma', *Business Day*, 31 July 2013. Minister of Basic Education Angie Motshekga is a powerful Zuma ally. She heads the ANC Women's League. At the time there had been a widespread call for her resignation due primarily to the Limpopo textbook crisis. In his cabinet shuffle (see note 39), Zuma took no action against her. He said elsewhere that she was doing an 'excellent job'.

and I cannot discuss their performance in public. It is my
responsibility to protect their integrity and that information.' [41]

2014

'I heard this white person saying let there be an investigation,
they can't pass like this, and I said to myself, this person still
has that old mentality that black people are not intelligent, if
they succeed it must be probed.' [42]

'We are approaching the elections as enthusiastically as we
were when we approached the 2009 elections and certainly
I can tell you we are going to deliver even better, with or
without Vavi or whoever else.' [43]

'Well, he was in the ANC, he was under particular discipline
and I saw in him potential and, I told him so as well – that
there were some rough edges that needed to be smoothed.
Unfortunately we did not have time to do so and he is now
no longer in the ANC, I can't be saying exactly the same thing.
Because the very fact that in the ANC you cause problems
until you are expelled, it means the ANC could not put you
right. I can't therefore say exactly the same thing I said then.' [44]

---

41. Ibid. Zuma's explanation for his lack of an explanation (see note 39). He was,
however, happy to discuss the merits of the cabinet member's performance at
great length; for that, a different rule seemed to apply (see note 40).

42. Speaking to supporters in Kanyamazane, Mpumalanga. 'Zuma lays into "white"
Zille', *Cape Argus*, 9 January 2014. Zuma was taking issue with Zille's suggestion
that the 2013 matric results be investigated because the outcomes were at
significant variance with previous trends.

43. 'Zuma talks Nkandla, Malema, Guptagate', eNCA, 16 February 2014.

44. Ibid. Asked about Julius Malema and his remark (see note 35) that Malema was
someone who, Zuma had said, showed leadership potential.

'Don't listen to people who, yesterday, told us their blood
was ANC DNA. How can we trust people who change their
allegiance daily? We will rule until someone who came before
returns ... Anybody who starts a political party now
is abnormal. Maybe we didn't realise this when they were in
the ANC. No one who is normal can think there's another party
that can win the elections other than the ANC. That person is
abnormal.'[45]

'In my honest view I doubt that Cosatu will split. I doubt it.
There may be a small sliver that could go away ... but I don't
think that this now is a disaster.'[46]

---

45. Addressing over 2 000 ANC supporters and volunteers at Ga-Rankuwa Stadium.
'Zuma takes swipe at "abnormal" Julius Malema', *City Press*, 7 March 2014. Zuma
manages to allude to Jesus's supposed return and Malema in one statement.

46. 'Jacob Zuma shrugs off jeers and is confident ahead of polls', *Financial Times*,
9 March 2014. Zuma shrugs off discontent in the ANC's alliance partner, the
Congress of South African Trade Unions, battling both the suspension of its
secretary general (and long-time Zuma-supporter-turned-enemy) Zwelinzima Vavi
and the trade union the National Union of Metalworkers South Africa, which
vowed not to support the ANC in the 2014 elections.

A MAN FOR ALL
SEASONS

JACOB ZUMA AND ANC POLICY

'Policies are not like the Ten Commandments.'

Time and time again, Jacob Zuma has gone out of his way to stress that it is not he who advocates any given policy, but the ANC, on whose behalf he speaks. He put it like this in a 2009 interview: 'I am leader of the ANC because ANC members consider that I believe in the ANC's principles', before elaborating that '[m]y duty as ANC president is to promote ANC policy. I cannot promote my policy'.

Zuma argued that '[p]eople are mistaken in attributing policies to individuals when they do not correspond to individuals. They are actually ANC policy'. That is all well and good when dodging a difficult question or, in the face of some controversy, hiding behind 'collective responsibility'. But the truth is that he has advocated a raft of positions that seem entirely of his own creation, particularly during the golden period of general appeasement that ranged from the run-up to his election as ANC president in Polokwane to his election as South African president in April 2009.

That period perhaps best captures Zuma the populist. Throughout 2008, he tried desperately to be all things to all people. In every chapter of this book, that year stands out like a beacon. It was when he was at his most confident: Mbeki had been defeated, his rape trial was behind him, and, with his hands on formal power for the first time, he must have had some sense of control over his legal battles with corruption for the first time too. He may not have been South African president yet, but real power was in his grasp as he controlled the ANC.

Not yet weighed down by the burden of having been elected president of South Africa, he could wax lyrical about every issue under the sun. He could be for affirmative action and express reservations about it, only later to call for its intensification; question labour laws and then support them, and advocate a referendum on the death penalty but then say he was misunderstood. At the very height of his confidence, he could even suggest that his preference was for a single term as president, expediently differentiating himself from Mbeki in the public eye.

He could also play Mbeki's weaknesses off against his own deference to the hive mind that was the ANC. Mbeki's position on HIV/Aids, for example, was painted as his own, personal pursuit, not ANC policy – even though Zuma himself had risen many times in Parliament to defend Mbeki. At this time, Mbeki's administration was, as Zuma himself would put it, a 'dead snake'. There may have been no point in beating it, but that didn't stop Zuma from having the occasional bash at it anyway.

How much of this was naivety is hard to say. As president, he seemed genuinely frustrated by how slowly the government worked when it came to dealing with corruption, for example – something he had promised to speed up. Some of it, no doubt, was attributed to his being less accountable and constrained by a hyper-scrutinising press, which would later place his every word under a powerful microscope. What remains was attributable to the impulse to accommodate, as far as possible, all and sundry.

Riding on a brief wave of popularity, he spent time explaining ad nauseam to the many journalists to whom he spoke how the ANC worked – how its policies were the result of internal debate and how it always seemed to arrive at the right decision. The lack of ethical or moral conviction that Zuma has displayed when dealing with corruption or personal scandal is evident, too, in the manner in which he defers to the collective wisdom of the party to which he is so loyal. It is robotic, almost – as if he is merely the amplifier for a signal he receives from Luthuli House.

Nevertheless, Zuma's personality materialised in his words and undertakings – each of which the press latched onto as proof either of a radical new agenda that was the cause for much concern, or of the assurance that continuity would prevail and that the country was in safe hands. Looking back, one can only wonder: what happened to all the promise that Zuma used to exude?

Zuma, the ANC and his policies

1999

'We realised from 1994 that when we went into government
there was no strategising in terms of deploying our cadres
in every respect. We acknowledged that in the conference in
1994 in Bloemfontein in the political report that Mandela gave.
In Mafikeng we still recognised it and took a decision that it
is important for the ANC to look at its cadres because other
people would leave government and go to the private sector
at will and none of them were trained by the ANC. We needed
to sit here and say where do we deploy our best cadres where
they could make the best impact in terms of transformation,
in terms of delivery? We needed to help the leaders, the
government as a majority party, to say here's a reservoir of
cadres and we need to have a view also.'[1]

'It's not to say, in the Afrikaner, for example, they were not
putting the NP members per se, they were putting Afrikaners.
We are putting ANC's, not a race. In the ANC there are
Afrikaners, some of them are occupying key positions, there
are Indians, there are English speaking and we look at the

---

1. Interview with Jacob Zuma. 'The Heart of Hope', available online at http://www.
nelsonmandela.org/omalley/index.php/site/q/03lv00017/04lv00344/05lv01258/06
lv01352.htm, 15 December 1999. The excerpt is significant because it is, to my
knowledge, the only meaningful discussion about cadre deployment ever had
with Zuma, or any senior ANC leader for that matter. Initially Zuma downplays
what is set down in black and white in the various ANC discussion documents on
the subject, suggesting that the idea is merely about getting the right person for
the job but, as the interview progresses, it becomes apparent that its purpose is
far more hegemonic and designed to blur not just the line between party and state
but, indeed, the line between the party and society itself.

quality, we look at their merits. That's why we find them everywhere. Then it was racialism. That's the difference, they were putting race for an evil agenda, only Afrikaners. Not even the whites per se, not a political approach, it was the Afrikaners who have been put in places and moving everybody else. So it's totally different to this.'[2]

2003

'[T]he labour laws that we have are indeed conducive to job creation. I think that for the first time we have laws that take into account workers in a very serious manner. I don't think we can fault the laws. There are other factors that relate to the increase in unemployment or whatever, not the labour laws. The labour laws are very user-friendly for the most disadvantaged group of our people, the workers. Therefore they cannot be associated with creating unemployment. If anything, they create better employment for the workers, and that is what they are aimed at doing.'[3]

2008

'Thus even the minimum wage therefore buys very much

---

2. 'The Heart of Hope'. O'Malley ends with the assertion (which is entirely correct, in my opinion) that such a programme is no different from what the National Party practised under apartheid. Zuma's response, typically obtuse, is to suggest that, because ANC members are of all races, the comparison is not fair. This is wrong, of course. Both programmes are about power and control. The Nats happened to deploy only white Afrikaners because they were racist. That the ANC should deploy members of any race says nothing about its purpose: to control, influence and direct all levers of power in South Africa, whether independent, public or private, with or without elected authority.

3. Answering questions in the National Assembly. Hansard, 2 April 2003, p. 881. One of many staunch defences offered by Zuma in the face of criticism of South Africa's labour laws and spiralling unemployment. As with many of his positions, he has contradicted it more recently. See his 2008 quote (referenced by note 4).

high – does not consider the second economy. Even the trade unions that say we stand for the workers but the workers that belong there, the unemployed, can't reach the bar. So that's a contradiction which we need to address because there is no regulation that says "how do we make the two link?" It's not flexibility – that's what we need to deal with. It's not just a question of the trade unions only – the trade unions are a reflection of the first economy and they have to pick up their level to that level so the second economy is in fact neglected by all of us.'[4]

'We need to look at policy. Policies are not like the Ten Commandments. Policies are made by people, and if in the process of implementation you see faults and mistakes, deal with it so that it does not create unnecessary problems.'[5]

'I don't think affirmative action was introduced to victimize other people – it's not the objective. If people are being victimized, the policy should be urgently debated – because some people may not be aware of how this affects other people. Once we discover that, let us address it … we should not have a young man who is going to grow up despondent, feeling that when he grows up he won't be able to participate.'[6]

---

4. 'Drawing the BEE sting', *Financial Mail*, 15 February 2008. An about-turn from his 2003 position.

5. Speech to members of the trade union Solidarity, 7 March 2008. Solidarity is vehemently opposed to affirmative action and this quote was widely interpreted as an attempt by Zuma to suggest a loosening of the regulatory framework governing the policy. It was not to be, however; like many statements Zuma made in the run-up to his election, it seemed rather to be further evidence that he was trying to be all things to all people.

6. Ibid.

'No, no, no, no, no, that was the view of President Mbeki.'[7]

'The ANC and South Africa cannot go the Zimbabwean way ...
[although I] cannot sit here and judge my colleagues in
Zanu–PF, the ANC has a different culture. The ANC believes
in collective leadership.'[8]

'There will be no Zanufication here.'[9]

'It's a very painful situation. I am one of those who think
we could have done things differently. Those who served in
the [apartheid] police force and in the old army have their
pensions. But it was made very difficult for those who fought
for freedom. They have been pushed from pillar to post.'[10]

'As South Africans we are not the kind of people who hate our
neighbours. We are very warm people.'[11]

'One of the things I would want to be able to do in
government, is to find a way of shortening the time of delivery
in government. That at times makes me sick, when you have
a situation [where] something could be done in two/three
months. I don't understand the logic.'[12]

---

7. Zuma reassuring the journalist that, were he elected president, he would
    not adopt President Mbeki's approach to HIV and Aids. 'Zuma is a "a man of
    contradictions"', *The Citizen*, 7 April 2008.

8. 'SA will not become another Zimbabwe', *Sowetan*, 29 May 2008.

9. Ibid.

10. 'We could have done more and we can still do more', *Sowetan*, 30 May 2008.
    About MK military veterans.

11. Ibid. Zuma in response to the spate of xenophobic attacks that South Africa
    was suffering at the time.

12. 'I want just one term', *Sunday Independent*, 27 July 2008.

'We need to introduce a kind of management style that … must bring the political consciousness that must say: "if I lead a department, I should not be a traditional leader of a department and say my department must have everything" … so that there is no jealously … Ministers must understand that … if there is a lack of performance we must be able to discuss it.'[13]

'We have to accept that tenders have caused a problem and therefore [ask whether] the systems that are being used are adequate and correct.'[14]

'We need to move with speed. There must be a cooling-off period so that we don't have a situation which advantages other people unfairly … It must not also totally disadvantage people.'[15]

'I don't think it's right to judge people, as there are certain circumstances in different countries that evolve, but in the same breath I think Mugabe has overstayed his position. There were no limits in terms of his leadership. That is the problem with a person who stays in power too long – you become a power unto yourself.'[16]

---

13. 'I want just one term', *Sunday Independent*, 27 July 2008.

14. Ibid.

15. Ibid. About people moving from politics into business.

16. 'Zumafication of our nation', *Leadership*, 1 September 2008. This quote is suited to this chapter because it illustrates that the exception proves the rule. This position was essentially an aberration, entirely inconsistent with the approach that the ANC, the government and Zuma had taken to Mugabe in the past and the position that Zuma's administration adopted towards him after Zuma was elected president. Indeed, if there is no such thing as individual policy, but only the ANC's collective mindset (as Zuma has repeatedly claimed), this would represent a significant breach of protocol on Zuma's part because nowhere has the ANC endorsed or expressed this view.

2009

'No, I don't think so.' [17]

'Mbeki raised a view which he continued to say was his view. He posed the question whether HIV caused Aids. It was not the policy of the ANC, nor the policy of government. People should distinguish between Mbeki's opinions and government policies, which were comprehensive. There was too much politicking over HIV and Aids. If you were to say, was that a shortcoming? No, because we never said we agreed with Mbeki's view.' [18]

'In the process of this, what I noticed as a result of what was happening to me is that there were laws that were introduced in parliament which … you felt there [*sic*] were actually aimed at dealing with the criminals. Only, you realised later, they were actually meant to make Madiba feel the way he was feeling. We need to remove that, we need to make South Africans feel if I am not a criminal, nobody is listening to me as I talk. Therefore we are going to find a way not only of dealing with this in terms of declaration [but] even to look at the law.' [19]

---

17. In response to the question whether the ANC should punish Thabo Mbeki, who was effectively guilty of 'slaughter by omission' through his various Aids policies. 'Jacob Zuma: a child of the ANC', *Sunday Independent*, 22 February 2009.

18. Ibid.

19. Saying that he aimed to change South Africa's surveillance laws, which, he felt, his opponents were misusing against him. 'I will change South Africa's Gestapo surveillance laws, says Zuma', *Cape Argus*, 9 April 2009. He introduced his undertaking with the following story: 'I went to see President Mandela in Maputo one day, it was after the case was thrown out of court in Pietermaritzburg (September 2006). There was a time when he wanted to make a sensitive point, he then called for pen and paper and wrote and gave it to me [to] read. I'm telling you I've never felt the pain as I felt at that point. Because I said to myself, what are we doing in our country? Here is a man who suffered for his freedom, he is afraid of it. He thinks and believes he is being listened to. And I said are we in a Gestapo state?'

'The fact of the matter is the ANC does not look at things from a race point of view ... We never looked at things in terms of race an ethnicity but in terms of non-racialism as South Africans.' [20]

2010

'Within government we have measures in place that regulate members of the executive as well as public servants with regards to the disclosure of business interests, gifts and assets. We are always looking at ways and means of making these measures more effective and that is why we recently appointed an inter-ministerial committee to fight corruption.' [21]

'I think the sense of urgency in government is very much alive.' [22]

'I have concerns that government moves very slowly.' [23]

---

20. 'Zuma opposes call for debate on race', *The Star*, 14 August 2009. Zuma may claim as much but the truth is that the ANC places a heavy emphasis on race and ethnicity only to ensure equality. Asked about the ethnic breakdown of the cabinet, ANC Secretary General Gwede Mantashe told the *Sunday Times* on 30 June 2013 that it was the result of a 'conscious decision by the ANC leadership, to achieve a balanced distribution' and that the result was not achieved by the 'sole choice of the President'.

21. Address to the Parliamentary Press Gallery. 'Zuma rejects Vavi's call for lifestyle audits', *Business Day*, 24 February 2010. Zuma's rejection, as with so many of his statements, was not without irony or contradiction. Just a few months later, on 21 April 2010, the public protector found that Zuma's declaration of his financial interests to Parliament 'constituted partial compliance with section 5 of the Executive Ethics Code' and that there was 'a systemic pattern of noncompliance with the timelines and some of the requirements stipulated in the code by a substantial number of members of the executive, which should be attended to by the Cabinet urgently'. Worth comparing, too, with Zuma's 2008 call for a 'cooling-off period'.

22. 'We do things slowly in government', *City Press*, 2 May 2010. This quote, in response to the question, 'What is your take on the state of government?' after Zuma's first year in office, is remarkable mainly for the quote that follows directly below, which Zuma made in the same interview, just one question later.

23. Ibid. In response to the question, 'Are there any areas of concern for you?'

'There is no law that debars the ANC in establishing
Chancellor House and Chancellor House investing. What
I have heard, particularly the opposition talking about, are
moral questions. The question of the ANC trying to raise
money for itself is a decision that was taken otherwise there
would be no Chancellor House. To me the question is why
this issue is raised as though the ANC has broken the law.'[24]

2012

'Here we are introducing a culture that looks at things
differently. We must not think we are the worst – in Parliament
we even discuss intelligence – that doesn't happen in other
democracies. We are a unique democracy.'[25]

2014

'We must therefore intensify the implementation of affirmative
action policies in order to deepen reconciliation and social
cohesion in our country.'[26]

---

24. 'We do things slowly in government'. In response to a question asking Zuma to
    clarify the ANC's position on its investment arm, Chancellor House. DA leader
    Helen Zille said of Chancellor House, in March 2014: 'Hitachi Power Africa is
    the company that got contracts of R38 billion to install boilers at the Medupi
    and Kusile power stations, right here in Mpumalanga ... Chancellor House, the
    investment arm of the ruling party announced on Friday that it sold its 25% stake
    in Hitachi Power Africa, which had controversially benefited from state-funded
    contracts. The shares in the Japanese firm's African subsidiary were sold to
    Hitachi Power Europe for an undisclosed amount.' The ANC had, she said,
    'controversially benefited from state-funded contracts'.

25. Answering a question about the Protection of State Information Bill. 'His master's
    loud voice', *City Press*, 12 February 2012. Of course, Zuma is wrong; in many
    other democracies, intelligence is discussed far more openly and in far more
    detail than it is discussed in South Africa.

26. Address by President Jacob Zuma in response to the debate on the State of the
    Nation Address, National Assembly, 20 February 2014. Worth comparing to his
    2008 equivocations on affirmative action.

ODDS AND ENDS

JACOB ZUMA AND
RANDOM CONTROVERSY

'I'm sure many of those heads of state have been booed at one point or the other.'

One can explain many of Zuma's controversial statements by referring to his personal convictions or political nature, but many fall outside of these, the primary impulses that define him. These are the remarks made because they seemed politically expedient at the time, were the consequence of a general, unthinking superficiality, or were merely cases of rhetoric fumbling in the dark.

No politician anywhere in the world has a spotless record on this front, but some do lend themselves to controversy more readily than others. Those who excel at regularly offending people tend to be: (1) ahistorical (they have no real memory of past positions or, indeed, of history itself, and thus often contradict themselves); (2) unable to think on their feet (unscripted questions usually stump them or inadvertently reveal hidden bias); and/or (3) given to talking in generalisations and platitudes (so that anything specific stands out markedly, attracting both attention and scrutiny).

Zuma is all three of these things, and is not helped by
a general discomfort with the English language. Often,
his most controversial statements are made in isiZulu;
when he does overstep the mark in English, it sometimes
appears that he lacks a rich enough vocabulary to express
subtlety or ambiguity, which, when expressed in absolute
terms, takes on a life of its own.

Many argue that this linguistic barrier hides a man who
is far more sophisticated than his public errors suggest.
This, however, is doubtful. Zuma could perhaps escape
some of the blunter contradictions and confusion for
which he is responsible if he could only speak in his first
language. But, in repeating many of his contradictions
so often (his religious or cultural beliefs, for example),
he makes it clear that a consistent sentiment underpins
them all. Regardless of one's mastery of language, in politics it is next to impossible to hide one's authentic convictions indefinitely. Sooner or later they will out.

Zuma's great skill lies behind the public political
scene – in the art of engendering loyalty, controlling
factional threats or interests, and mobilising favourable
sentiment. At these, he is a ruthless adversary. But ask
him to articulate a vision or ideal in a compelling way and
you will wait in vain. Zuma's behind-the-scenes skill is

unfortunately accompanied by a front-of-house shambles; in that regard, words are his biggest enemy.

There is an upside to being generally oblivious to contradiction and doublespeak – do it often enough, and the public tends to forgive more quickly than it would a great wordsmith or interlocutor. It becomes, simply, par for the course. The public may respond with temporary outrage but, generally, each blunder is assigned to the pile of 'inevitable mishaps', quickly forgotten when the next gaffe hits the headlines. There have been weeks and months in which Zuma has moved seamlessly from one controversy to the next, each one assigned to the political scrapheap by the media as soon as he articulates the next one.

This may be convenient for the perpetrator – indeed, former ANC Youth League leader Julius Malema thrives on this kind of one-week media amnesia – but to those who care about consistency, transparency and justification, such a person's record reveals little more than a mass of unexplained, unsolved riddles, never contextualised.

And so it is with Zuma. Most politicians aspire to leave a legacy of great speeches and visionary statements. Outside of controversy, Zuma's legacy will be a bland, lifeless and amorphous collection of nothings, interspersed with baffling political blunders.

A curious collection of Zuma controversies

Timeless

'... *khawuleth'umshini wami*
Wen'uyang'ibambezela
umshini wami, khawuleth'umshini wami'[1]

2000

'Why would I be any different from other South Africans? I am a South African. I am part of this country. I must be judged by that standard. If and when I want to make my status known, I shall do so.'[2]

2001

'From our point of view we are happy. From our point of view we are confident. We think we are doing our best with our capacity and we are making progress.'[3]

---

1. The last three lines of the ANC struggle song, *Awuleth' Umshini Wami* or 'Bring me my machine gun'. The three lines translate as: 'Please bring my machine / You're pulling me back / My machine, please bring my machine'. This song has caused Zuma and many others much trouble and it has followed him around throughout his political career, as have many others. The call for a weapon has offended many, who argue it is inappropriate language for a state president; but Zuma routinely turns to it, a crowd favourite and by some distance his signature rallying call.

2. 'Geen rede vir hom om sy vigsstatus te onhul, sê Zuma', *Beeld*, 19 May 2000. An entirely valid point made by Zuma, in refusing to disclose his status – except, as with so many Zuma positions, it did change over time. In May 2010, he launched the government's HIV-testing campaign by disclosing his status and said in an interview, 'I announced my status to help people psychologically to see that this is not a death sentence.' See 'We do things slowly in government', *City Press*, 2 May 2010.

3. At the height of the Mbeki Aids controversy and in response to a Human Rights Watch report that accused Mbeki of negligence on the issue. 'We are tackling Aids, says Zuma', *Pretoria News*, 23 November 2001. Zuma would also say that '[i]t is also easy to [be critical] when you do a report about other people. I am not sure if you take developing countries which one would compare with South Africa in so far as fighting HIV/Aids'. The irony of that statement was obviously lost on him.

2002

'We have deliberated with Mokaba on his several utterances, including the AIDS issue and his questions of the continued existence of the ANC/Cosatu/SACP alliance, and we are content his position on AIDS has not had a tremendous bearing on our AIDS strategy.'[4]

2003

'South Africa would certainly not persuade Saddam Hussein to leave his country. This would be a wrong move. We cannot determine what happens to the leaders of other countries. It is the people of those countries who have a right to change their leaders. It is important to observe and respect the sovereignty of other countries and to go into exile.'[5]

2005

'If I was guilty – if I knew I at any time was guilty – I am sure I would have made it as easy as anything.'[6]

---

4. 'Zuma reprimands Mokaba', *City Press*, 12 May 2002. Hardly a reprimand. ANC Youth League leader Peter Mokaba had told the *New York Times* in an interview, 'HIV? It doesn't exist. The kind of stories that they tell that people are dying in droves … It's not true. It's not borne out by any facts. Where the science has not proved anything, we cannot allow our people to be guinea pigs. Antiretrovirals, they're quite dangerous. They're poison actually. We cannot allow our people to take something so dangerous that it will exterminate them. However well-meaning, the hazards of misplaced compassion could lead to genocide.' This was a typically technocratic, rather than moral response from Zuma. The word 'tremendous' is also significant.

5. Answering questions in the National Assembly. Hansard, 2 April 2003, p. 885. The logic behind silent diplomacy taken to its ultimate conclusion. It is one thing to have the right to vote, but quite another when one is prevented from exercising that right. Interestingly, just nine months earlier (in July 2002) Aziz Pahad and the Department of Foreign Affairs hosted Iraq's Deputy Prime Minister Tariq Aziz (since a convicted war criminal). Aziz met Mbeki and, significantly, addressed an ANC meeting.

6. In an interview with SABC Africa. 'Why I would not quit – Zuma', *Sunday Independent*, 19 June 2005. Zuma has been forced to answer the question of whether he will resign many, many times in his political career. This answer perhaps best sums up all of his answers.

2006

'My trip to Libya was private. If I go to Libya on private matters, does it mean I am getting money from Gaddafi? I suppose that the next time I fly privately to London, I will be said to be getting financial assistance from the queen.'[7]

'With regard to HIV/Aids, I have advocated prevention, care, treatment and support in various forms over the years, I shall continue to do so both as president … as the deputy president of the ANC … and as an ordinary citizen.'[8]

2008

'Umshini wami belongs to the ANC. Who are these people abusing this song while they are doing wrong things? They are abusing the names of ANC leaders in the process … criminals are sparking these xenophobic attacks and some political organisations are also perpetuating this – I don't know how true this is.'[9]

'We took a resolution on the Scorpions and allowed the country to debate the matter. Why should that not be the case with the Springboks?'[10]

7. 'Wily old soldier keeps his council', *Sunday Argus*, 14 May 2006. It was alleged that Zuma had funded his rape trial defence through money from the late Libyan despot Muammar Gaddafi. He flew to Libya 12 days after being charged and faced a legal bill of some R12 million.

8. Just after being acquitted of rape. 'Zuma's "when I'm president" was telling', *Daily Dispatch*, 10 May 2006. A significant slip of the tongue for a man who constantly claims to have no personal ambition and who serves only at the ANC's behest.

9. 'Umshini isn't a song to kill, says Zuma', *Independent Online*, 19 May 2008. Available online at http://www.iol.co.za/news/politics/umshini-isn-t-a-song-to-kill-says-zuma-1.400935#.UyX9EdzaMpE. After a spate of xenophobic attacks, in which it was reported that some culprits sang Zuma's trademark song (see note 1).

10. 'Zuma calls for debate on the Springbok', *Weekend Argus* (Saturday Edition), 8 November 2008. In a September 2008 interview, not two months earlier, Zuma had said in response to the question, 'Springboks or All Blacks?', 'I could never support anyone but my own country! The Springboks of course! I actually watched the semi-finals against Argentina at the World Cup and absolutely loved it.'

2009

'Of all the white groups that are in South Africa, it is only the Afrikaners that are truly South Africans in the true sense of the word.'[11]

2011

'There is a trend across the world where former leaders accused of injustice are not given an opportunity to stand trial in a court of justice. That is surprising. I think even those who accused him [Gaddafi] would have wanted to see him become answerable.'[12]

2012

'Our call to teachers to be in school, in class, on time, teaching for at least seven hours a day remains pivotal to success. We thank the teacher unions for supporting this campaign.'[13]

---

11. To a group of agricultural, women's and cultural organisations at the Hilton Hotel in Sandton, Johannesburg. 'Zuma: "It's only the Afrikaners who are truly South African"', *Mail & Guardian*, 3 April 2009. The comment caused some consternation but the *M&G* headline is somewhat deceptive because, while Zuma was clearly electioneering ahead of the 2009 national elections, he hadn't said that Afrikaners were the only true South Africans, only the only true South African grouping of white people in the country. Divisive, nonetheless.

12. 'Gaddafi should have been captured – Zuma', South African Press Association, 21 October 2011. Zuma, a long-time ally of Gaddafi, from whom it was rumoured he had received funds to pay for his rape trial defence, responding to Gaddafi's death.

13. 'State of the Nation Address by His Excellency Jacob G Zuma, President of the Republic of South Africa on the occasion of the Joint Sitting of Parliament', 9 February 2012. Zuma's remark, seemingly an endorsement of the South African Democratic Teachers Union, was rounded upon by DA leader Helen Zille who said that '[t]he conduct of Sadtu over the last two years is nothing short of a national disgrace. It deserves censure from every leader, of every party. To see President Zuma so flippantly thank Sadtu in his State of the Nation Address was to witness political expediency in its worst form.' Presidency spokesperson Mac Maharaj said in response that Zille's claim was a 'gross fabrication and distortion'.

'We cannot go back to the period or memory of Number 4 prison, where black men were made to strip naked and perform the "tauza" dance. Nor do we want to re-open the wounds of the humiliation of Sarah Baartman, who was painfully exhibited in London and Paris, and whose genitals and brain were stored in a pickle jar and shown off in a museum until the administration led by President Mandela demanded the return of her remains for a decent burial. We dare not repeat that painful, brutal, primitive treatment of a human being.' [14]

'You are dealing with a teacher that comes from the Verwoerdian system … his or her attitude towards education still needs to be worked on. We are not dealing with a problem of today; we are solving a problem of centuries [ago].' [15]

'There will be individuals who think differently. I don't think in a country you can have people thinking and feeling exactly the same. I think it is [that] people have got their own ideas, they want to express them. I might have a view about it, but some people might have a different view about it. I thought it was rather vulgar. Particularly if you portray a particular person [that way], but of course I think the population did express itself at that time, which will tell you it is not everybody who approved of it. I think in fact the majority did not approve of

14. Address by President Jacob Zuma on the occasion of the reply to the Presidency Budget Vote Debate, National Assembly, 31 May 2012. An obscure reference to the Brett Murray painting *The Spear*, which Zuma believed violated his dignity.

15. In an interview on 567 CapeTalk/Radio 702 with Redi Tlhabi, 23 July 2012. Zuma was asked about a textbook crisis in Limpopo, in which the provincial government had failed during the course of the year to deliver thousands of textbooks to hundreds of schools in the province. His apartheid excuse, used so often to explain so much, generated massive outrage. A long-lasting debate ensued in the media.

it … Some white people, for example, thought that was not helpful to deal with the race issue in the country.' [16]

'Now you can't say the minister of police is responsible for that, to start the thing. When the workers were striking, they had every other kind of weapon in their hands. In fact, long before the shooting, 10 people had died, including two policemen, two security policemen. How many other people would have died if, for example, police did not move to disarm these people? Nobody can tell. At a spur of the moment, a mistake happened. Now if such a mistake happened, you throw the minister away? I don't know on what basis.' [17]

2013

'To suggest we cannot blame apartheid for what is happening in our country now, I think is a mistake to say the least. We don't need to indicate what it is apartheid did. The fact that the country is two in one, you go to any city, there is a beautiful part and squatters on the other side, this is not the making of democracy and we can't stop blaming those who caused it.' [18]

---

16. 'Jacob Zuma says Marikana killings a wake-up call on workers' conditions', *The Guardian* (UK), 13 December 2012. On Brett Murray's painting *The Spear*. He was asked in a wide-ranging interview, 'What does "The Spear" say about South Africa today?'

17. Ibid. On why the Minister of Safety and Security should not be fired over the Marikana massacre in which 34 miners were shot dead by police during a protest that turned violent. Marikana became the subject of national commission of inquiry.

18. Said at a wreath-laying ceremony in Ekurhuleni for slain SACP leader Chris Hani. 'We CAN blame apartheid, says Zuma', *The Star*, 11 April 2013. Following his comments about apartheid almost a year earlier (see note 15), Minister for National Planning in the Presidency Trevor Manuel had reignited the debate about the extent to which apartheid can be blamed for current service delivery failures, when he said that '[w]e can no longer say it is apartheid's fault … There is no longer a Botha regime looking over our shoulder, we are responsible ourselves.' This was Zuma's response.

'He is looking very good, he is in good shape. We had some
conversation with him, shook hands, he smiled … The doctors
are happy and we are happy. The report corresponded with his
own appearance as we saw it. So we are very happy about it.' [19]

2014

'I didn't take it as a big issue because that's part of democratic
politics … I'm sure many of those heads of state have been
booed at one point or the other.' [20]

'There is no president in the DA. She must ask other premiers
at her level to have a debate.' [21]

---

19. Outside Nelson Mandela's private house in Sandton. 'A glimpse of Madiba', eNCA,
    29 April 2013. The ANC undertook a visit to an ailing Nelson Mandela, less than
    eight months before he passed away. They invited television cameras into his
    house and pictures of a wincing, frail Mandela were rounded upon by the media
    and public alike. ANC spokesperson Jackson Mthembu said that the ANC 'had to
    show Mandela was alive'. Mandela's former wife, Winnie Madikizela-Mandela, said
    the visit was 'insensitive'. She said, 'I honestly can't put into words how hurt the
    family was.' One month later, Mandela was admitted to hospital, for the last time.

20. 'Jacob Zuma shrugs off jeers and is confident ahead of polls', *Financial Times*,
    9 March 2014. Zuma in response to the booing he had to endure on international
    television during the memorial service for former President Nelson Mandela, at
    the FNB Stadium, Soweto, in December 2013.

21. 'Zille not senior enough to debate: Zuma', eNCA News, 16 March 2014. In an open
    letter DA leader Helen Zille had challenged Zuma to a debate, ahead of the 2014
    elections. This was his response. By its logic, no presidential debate could ever
    take place anywhere, because there is only ever one sitting president.